T0383935

The Project Manager's Guide to Health Information Technology Implementation

The Project Manager's Guide to Health Information Technology Implementation

Third Edition

Susan M. Houston
MBA, RN-BC, PMP,
CPHIMS, FHIMSS

Routledge
Taylor & Francis Group

A PRODUCTIVITY PRESS BOOK

First published 2022
by Routledge
600 Broken Sound Parkway #300, Boca Raton FL, 33487

and by Routledge
2 Park Square, Milton Park, Abingdon, Oxon, OX14 4RN

Routledge is an imprint of the Taylor & Francis Group, an informa business

© 2022 Taylor & Francis

ISBN: 978-1-032-07388-0 (hbk)
ISBN: 978-1-032-07387-3 (pbk)
ISBN: 978-1-003-20666-8 (ebk)

DOI: 10.4324/9781003206668

Typeset in ITC Garamond Std
by KnowledgeWorks Global Ltd.

Contents

Preface... ix

Acknowledgments xi

Author xiii

1 What Is a Project?..1
  What Is a Project?..3
  Project Management..5

2 Project, Program, and Portfolio Management 9
  Project vs. Operations...9
  Program and Portfolio Management 10
  Case Study 1: Implementation of an Electronic Health Record 15
  Case Study 2: Implementation of a Research Tracking System...............15

3 Project Process Groups...17
  Initiating Process Group 19
  Planning Process Group 22
  Executing Process Group...26
  Monitoring and Controlling Process Group 27
  Closing Process Group...29
  Case Study 1: Implementation of an Electronic Health Record 30
  Case Study 2: Implementation of a Research Tracking System...............31

4 Project Knowledge Areas...33
  Integration Management 37
  Scope Management...38
  Schedule Management..39
  Cost Management..41
  Quality Management...42
  Resource Management 43

Communication Management...44
Risk Management..45
Procurement Management..47
Project Stakeholder Management 48
Case Study 1: Implementation of an Electronic Health Record 48
Case Study 2: Implementation of an Organizational Metrics
Dashboard..49

5 **Software Development Lifecycle**...**51**
Waterfall Model 55
Spiral Model 56
Rapid Prototype Model 56
Incremental Model 57
Agile Development..57
Commercial Off-the-Shelf (COTS) 58
Case Study 1: Implementation of an Electronic Health Record 60
Case Study 2: Implementation of an Organizational Metrics
Dashboard..61

6 **Agile Development Methodology**..**63**
The Agile Mindset...64
Agile Methods 65
Life Cycle Selection...66
Common Agile Practices and Terms 67

7 **Choosing the Right Methodology** **71**
JUDY WIGHT
What does "Methodology" Mean? 71
Why Is Choosing a Methodology Important? 72
Characteristics of Each Methodology 73
    Waterfall..73
    Agile..75
    Hybrid..77
What Factors Should the Project Manager Consider in
Choosing a Methodology?...79
    The Business 80
    Stakeholders, Customers, and Resources...81
    Project Characteristics 84
Discussion/Conclusion...86
Case Study 1: Implementation of an Electronic Health Record 88

Case Study 2: Implementation of an Organizational Metrics
Dashboard 89

8 Stakeholder Management 91
GRACE GALVEZ GONZALEZ
Stakeholder Identification 91
Stakeholder Analysis 94
Communication Plan 99
Stakeholder Management in Action 103
Case Study 1: Implementation of an Electronic Health Record 104
Case Study 2: Implementation of a Research Tracking System 104

9 System Configuration 107
Workstations 108
Client 108
Servers 109
Storage Area Network 110
Disaster Recovery 110
High Availability 112
Network 112
Interface 113
Environments 115
    Sandbox 115
    Development 116
    Test 116
    Preproduction 117
    Production 117
    Training 117
    Considerations 117
Case Study 1: Implementation of an Electronic Health Record 118
Case Study 2: Implementation of a Research Tracking System 119

10 Security and Privacy 121
BOB EICHLER
IT Project Security and Privacy Tasks 124
Case Study: Access to System by Outside Resources 131

11 Software Testing 133
Testing Types 135
Configuration and Release Management 139
Case Study 1: Implementation of an Electronic Health Record 141

Case Study 2: Implementation of an Organizational Metrics
Dashboard 142

12 Activation Management 143
  User Training 144
  Activation 146
  Activation Checklist 148
  Activation Rehearsal 150
  Case Study 1: Implementation of an Electronic Health Record 154
  Case Study 2: Implementation of a Research Tracking System 154

13 Project Transition to Support 155
  RYAN D. KENNEDY
  Why Does This Happen? 156
  Characteristics of a Support Center 157
  Change Management 159
  Managing Transition Throughout the Plan 160
  Initiating 160
  Planning 163
  Execution 167
  Closing 168
  Case Study 1: Implementation of an Electronic Health Record 171
  Case Study 2: Implementation of an Organizational Metrics
  Dashboard 171

14 Measuring Success 173
  PATRICIA P. SENGSTACK
  Case Study 1: Implementation of an Electronic Health Record 179
  Case Study 2: Implementation of an Organizational Metrics
  Dashboard 179

Appendix A: Case Study Feedback 181

Appendix B: Earned Value Management (EVM) 215

Appendix C: Forms and Templates 219

References and Additional Readings 253

Index 255

Preface

We are continuing in the direction of a paperless healthcare system. As organizations move down this path, information technology is becoming more important to providing healthcare with rapid changes occurring. One such change is the emergence of telehealth in response to the pandemic.

The different vendors are positioning themselves by offering more and more modules with a specific niche or purchasing other smaller companies to offer these products. Implementing an electronic health record (EHR) is only the beginning; there are unique needs in almost every department that will offer the question to make what we have fit or obtain another system to meet this need. Some feel that this is a never-ending cycle since the influx of cybersecurity concerns makes it even more important to continuously upgrade the systems you already have, while being asked to implement more.

With all of this comes the need for more project management and the understanding of what it takes to implement quality software that is secure and usable. Some software projects are large multiyear efforts to bring a full EHR to an organization, while others are the smaller niche systems for a few users. Some will be purchased from a company that developed the software for sale, while others will be built just for a single unique need.

It is important for project managers to have a toolkit where they can draw upon tools and concepts for each project they manage. Since each project is unique, the necessary tools will vary from one to the other. As project managers move through each project, they will gather more tools to add to their toolbox to be used in future projects.

This book provides essential concepts for any project manager who will be leading a project to implement healthcare information technology. The early chapters will provide a review for experienced project managers as well as an introduction for those new to the industry. The later chapters introduce concepts and define terms used for software implementation projects that will add more tools available for healthcare information technology projects.

A project manager is rarely an expert in the design, development, testing, training, or technical implementation of software, and this should not be the expectation. This book provides an overview of software and hardware concepts that will allow the project manager to understand the aspects of implementation projects. These chapters may not make you an expert in these areas, but it will provide guidance so the right questions are asked of those who are the experts for a successful project.

The third edition of this book brings about updates from the PMBOK sixth edition as well as some updates for new concepts that have arisen since the previous editions were published. Also, three chapters have been added to better round out the content. First is the timely topic of Agile management. While Agile has been discussed in previous editions, it is a rapidly growing framework for custom developed software and is further outlined in Chapter 6. The second new chapter is Choosing the Right Methodology. This chapter provides guidance on how to determine the best framework to match the unique project. When to use a more traditional waterfall model, an Agile model, or maybe tailoring the process to be a hybrid of multiple— all this is discussed in Chapter 7. The third new chapter provides an enhanced discussion on stakeholder management and communication planning. Stakeholder management is an important aspect of all projects, big or small, and communication is a large part of a project manager's role. These topics can be found in Chapter 8.

Susan M. Houston

Acknowledgments

I would like to thank everyone who supported me during the writing of this edition of the book. My husband, Gary, is my rock, whose patience and support never waivers. He is always there with thoughts, opinions, or sarcasm, depending on what is appropriate for the occasion. The rest of the family have always been there for encouragement or a much-needed distraction; thank you Nicole, Matt, Dana, and Nick. I know you are only a call, e-mail, or text away.

The contributions of Judy Wight, and Grace Gonzalez, for two of the new chapters were amazing and I appreciate your insights and ongoing friendship. A thank you to Bob Eichler, who stepped in to review the Security and Privacy chapter when Susan Martin was unavailable. He brought in some valuable and timely details to the chapter. I am grateful for the ongoing friendship, guidance, and support from Ryan Kennedy and Patricia Sengstack. My thanks and appreciation goes out to each of you.

A word of thanks to Nix, for the original and updated graphics used in the book.

Author

Susan M. Houston, MBA, RN-BC, PMP, CPHIMS, FHIMSS, has extensive clinical, informatics, and project, program, and portfolio management experience. Ms. Houston has certifications in Nursing Informatics from American Nurses Credentialing Center (ANCC); Project Management Professional (PMP) from Project Management Institute (PMI); and Certified Professional in Healthcare Information and Management Systems (CPHIMS) from Healthcare Information Management Systems Society (HIMSS). Her formal education includes a Bachelor of Science in nursing and a Master of Business Administration. She started working in an emergency room while in nursing school. After graduation, she continued to work in emergency medicine for more than 15 years, finishing as a nurse manager of a Level 2 trauma center. Ms. Houston was then asked to implement a clinical information system because she was one of the few nurses who were comfortable with computers. This began her career as a project manager implementing clinical, administrative, and research systems. She has also worked for a software vendor and as a consultant, implementing a wide range of applications and processes for a variety of healthcare organizations. Susan was on the faculty at the University of Maryland School of Nursing, Baltimore, where she taught an Information Technology Project Management course for the Master of Nursing Informatics program. Ms. Houston has presented at a number of local, national, and international conferences as well as co-authored a number of articles and books. Ms. Houston has retired from the National Institutes of Health, Clinical Center where she was the Chief, Portfolio Office. During this time, she developed a Project Management Office, mentored other project managers throughout the hospital, and was accountable for the lifecycle of systems, from initial request, implementation, and configuration management through to disposition. Ms. Houston is now a senior consultant providing healthcare information technology services.

Chapter 1

What Is a Project?

Of all the things I've done, the most vital is coordinating the talents
of those who work for us and pointing them toward a certain goal.

Walt Disney

The healthcare industry continues to go through significant change with the
ongoing conversion from paper to electronic and the need for everything to be
integrated. Current challenges for the industry range from outdated technology
to cyber threats, the need for interoperability, and the continuous need to keep
up with rapidly changing medical advances. As healthcare organizations have
an ever-expanding portfolio of applications, there is a need for an overall,
consistent approach to the implementation, support, and management of each.

While there are many types of software, this book will focus only on two
broad categories: commercial off-the-shelf (COTS) and custom developed.
Depending on the organization, these may both be implemented using the
same project management processes with some differences in the activities.
There has been an emergence of an Agile method for software development
which is more of an approach than the traditional methodology. This
method lends itself more to the custom developed software rather than the
COTS. Chapter 6 provides an overview of Agile, while Chapter 7 provides
some guidance on how to choose the right methodology for your project.

Software vendors develop COTS systems with the intention of selling them
to a range of customers whose organizational size and structure and whose
specific needs, results, and workflow can vary enormously. To accommodate
the diversity of their customer base, COTS are often generic in design and
highly configurable, allowing customers to make modifications to fit unique
workflows. The configuration is completed through tools provided by the

DOI: 10.4324/9781003206668-1

vendor. The amount of work needed to customize COTS software varies among systems and should not be viewed as a minor task.

Custom-developed software, on the other hand, is developed with a single organization or use in mind. This software is based on specific requirements to fit a specific need. The development is completed by using software development tools and requires specific skills with using the tools as well as the ability to take sometimes very general requirements and build something that will meet the need. This development can be done internally or can be contracted out to a software development company. The similarities and differences between these two projects will be reviewed throughout this book.

Basic project management concepts are reviewed in Chapter 2 through Chapter 4. While these chapters do not provide an in-depth study of project management, they will provide a review for experienced project managers, as well as an introduction for those new to the role.

The next chapters outline topics related to implementing software and include terminology and concepts that project managers will find useful during implementation of their software projects. While project managers are not expected to be subject matter experts (SMEs), if they understand the basic concepts and terminology, they will be better prepared to ask the right questions and ensure the best decisions are made based on discussions with the project team. Key concepts such as the development lifecycle, stakeholder management, security and privacy, testing options, configuration and change management, planning for activation, transition to support, and measuring your success are also reviewed.

Two case studies will span the book, allowing readers to apply concepts described in each chapter. All software projects are different. There are no right or wrong answers, but some choices are better than others. The project management methodology you adopt needs to be flexible and adaptable in order to fit the needs and complexity of the project and its organization.

TIP

Two case studies are provided with additional information provided at the end of each chapter along with a few chapter-specific questions. In Appendix A, response will be provided for each question. Please remember, each situation is unique, and there is no wrong answer. It is perfectly acceptable for your answer to not match the author's.

A Guide to the Project Management Body of Knowledge (PMBOK) Sixth Edition, published by the Project Management Institute, provides a framework of best practices for project management practitioners. PMBOK should be part of every project manager's toolkit as they tailor their methodology to fit the size and complexity of the project along with the culture of the organization. This book follows the PMBOK but provides additional insights for implementing software specific to healthcare.

TIP

- A project manager is not expected to be an SME.
- Each stakeholder brings a unique viewpoint to the project.

What Is a Project?

Understanding the definition of a project is an important first step to understanding project management. A project is a temporary activity that becomes progressively elaborated as you move through the lifecycle and it produces a unique product, service, or result. Because of these characteristics, a project is different from a process. Implementing a new software system is a project, but so are some activities undertaken during the operations and maintenance of the same system, such as upgrading the hardware or software.

Because it is a temporary endeavor, a project has a defined beginning and end. A project begins when a need is identified and ends when the specific objectives are achieved and are formally accepted by the sponsor. A project can also end if a decision is made to terminate it prior to achieving the final outcome. This decision can be made for a number of reasons, such as determining that the objectives cannot be met, the need no longer exists, organizational priorities have changed, or resources are no longer available. Organizations should define what criteria are important for evaluating when to terminate a project.

The temporary nature of a project does not mean all projects last only a short about of time. Projects can last weeks or years, but irrelevant to the duration, every project goes through all phases of the project lifecycle. The amount of time spent in each of the phases will vary based on the amount of work required.

As projects are temporary endeavors, the project team is usually also temporary. Team members often work together for the purpose of the specific project only and, once the project ends, are released to return to other work or projects. A critical consideration for the project manager is that the members may not have worked together in the past. A focus on getting them to work as a team should begin as early as possible once the members have been identified. This is often accomplished through offsite social or team-building activities.

A project is developed in steps and continues in increments. Work is coordinated and detailed through a specific plan that is defined early and updated as more information is obtained. The plan includes a set of related tasks that are modified or expanded as the project progresses. Development begins with the broad scope and becomes more elaborate as functional requirements are defined; this is then followed by system design. The requirements and design are needed to help define the test phase, and the development feeds decisions around what to include in the training materials. For the traditional methodology, this process is very controlled and known during project planning. It is important to note that this elaboration is not the same as the uncontrolled aspect of scope creep. For the agile model, the process still includes defining requirements (called stories), design, development, and testing, but they are managed in a more iterative fashion.

A project produces a defined outcome such as a unique product, service, or result. Some projects may produce a combination of one or more of these outcomes. This final deliverable is what provides the guideline for when the project will be considered complete. As mentioned earlier, if it becomes apparent that the outcomes cannot be reached, the project should be terminated. Defining outcomes early in the project lifecycle also provides direction and boundaries for the rest of the project.

A product is a defined deliverable, such as new software to track the menus and diet orders for patients along with the ability to track the ordering and management of food supplies. In every case, a project comprises all of the work to create and deliver a unique product as in Figure 1.1.

A service is a deliverable that is less tangible than a product but supports a defined business function. Developing a new training program or workflow for patient transfers are examples of a service-focused project. It is important to note that the project is to develop or set up the service, not the ongoing effort of providing the service.

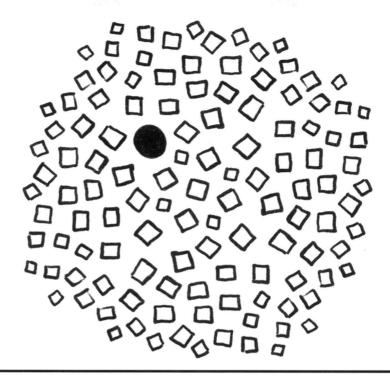

Figure 1.1   A unique product.

A project can also produce a specific result, such as conducting research. The presence of repeating elements, such as data collection, does not change the uniqueness of a project. The project begins with background research and a documented hypothesis and ends with the documented conclusion (i.e., a published article or presentation). In most cases, the conclusion, or increased knowledge, is the specific result that defines the end of the project. If this conclusion leads to further research, a new project will begin. The activity of system selection could be a project in itself where the actual selection decision is the result produced.

Project Management

There are many new to project management that might not understand the difference between project management, program management, and portfolio management. Project management will be defined here, while program management and portfolio management will be described in the next chapter.

Project management is the application of knowledge, skills, techniques and tools, and techniques to project activities to meet project requirements, according to PMBOK. It is accomplished through the application and incorporation of the project management processes, which will be defined in Chapter 3. There also are areas of knowledge that help define the management processes, which are required to successfully complete a project. These knowledge areas will be further defined in Chapter 4.

Ultimately, project management is a framework that defines how a project will be managed, and the project manager, by guiding each step of the framework, is responsible for the success or failure of the project. While these concepts are applicable for all projects, they are applied in more of an iterative manner for the agile methods, outlined in Chapter 6.

Based on the definition of a project provided earlier, project management differs from general management in a number of ways. The project team is brought together to complete a defined set of activities within a defined timeline. This demands that the project manager be able to build the team to work together within a finite period of time. This will invariably include what some call "micro-management." The project manager needs to know the status of all tasks, if there are any potential delays, and details of any issues or risks that might arise. Tracking this information is critical because the possibility of rapid change within projects requires the project manager to quickly adapt the plan in order to keep the project on time. A general manager, on the other hand, manages by exception; staff follows standard policies and procedures to complete their routine work.

A project manager must be able to focus on the daily details to ensure that the project stays on schedule while keeping an eye on the larger picture, to be proactive about how today's activities might impact tomorrow and adjust the plan accordingly. The need to conform tasks to deadlines and deliverables is more pronounced in project management than in general management.

Having a person with the right skill set in the project manager role is critical to success. Often, individuals are placed in this role because they understand the business processes, or they have the time to take on the project. However, if an individual does not have the right skills, he or she is simply being set up to fail. A good project manager must be able to lead the team and facilitate the completion of tasks or activities, all while communicating down to the team, up to the sponsors and organizational leadership, as well as out to all identified stakeholders.

In terms of the necessary skill set, although some feel subject matter knowledge is necessary, the project manager should not be expected to be a SME. Project managers should be able to manage any project as long as they have the right people on the team. With that said, it is often easier to understand the work being completed and to gain support from the team when the project manager has some knowledge related to the project. In the case of this book for example, the project manager should have a basic understanding of information technology (IT), software development, and healthcare. Table 1.1 illustrates some of the key skills of a project manager. Can you think of any others?

Project stakeholders are those who are actively involved or impacted by the project being undertaken. They can be project team members, sponsors, or others who exert influence on the project's deliverables or team from both internal and external to the organization. Stakeholders can be impacted positively or negatively by the project activities or deliverables. Stakeholders may find their staff reassigned to the project, have a change to their workflow, or get improved access to data. The project team should identify all stakeholders early in the project to properly evaluate their needs and expectations, since each stakeholder will have a unique perspective on the project. Chapter 8 provides more details on the identification, analysis, and management of stakeholders along with communication planning.

The project management process outlined in the next few chapters are designed to provide guidance on key concepts that should be included when managing projects of all types, sizes, and complexities. Since each project is unique, offers unique challenges, includes unique team member skills, and are done within a unique organizational culture, the project

Table 1.1 Key Skills for a Project Manager

Leadership	Facilitation
Communication	Collaboration
Critical thinking	Analytical thinking
Negotiation	Motivation
Decision making	Time management
Interpersonal skills	Project management process
Flexibility	Team management
General management	Organization

manager must be able to tailor the methodology to meet the current circumstances. Any project management methodology should be flexible enough to be tailored to the needs of the project. Guidelines should be in place to adapt the methodology to large or small projects, along with the minimum requirements. Implementing software follows the same concept. In this, each project will be different, and so, there is no single right or wrong answer for how to implement software. Tailoring can only occur if the project manager is knowledgeable of what is available and possible.

The concepts reviewed in this book are intended to provide a guide for the project manager to understand terminology and concepts, not to provide the level of detail required to make the reader a subject matter expert. It is also important to note that terminology within healthcare and information technology (IT) is not always clear or consistent. Each organization may utilize different terms for the same concepts, so it is highly recommended to ensure that you understand how terms are used in your organization.

Chapter 2

Project, Program, and Portfolio Management

Management is, above all, a practice where art, science, and craft meet.

Henry Mintzberg

The previous chapter provided an overview of project management. In this chapter, program management and portfolio management will be explained. While there are some characteristics that are similar between each, there are differences related to their specific functions and scope. These are summarized in Table 2.1, at the end of the chapter. A good starting point would be understanding the difference between a project and operations.

Project vs. Operations

Operations, sometimes referred to as operations and maintenance (O&M), is an ongoing process. As defined in the last chapter, projects are not ongoing but there are activities that occur during O&M that can be considered projects. These activities would need to meet the definition provided in Chapter 1. The activity of replacing hardware, upgrading the operating system, and implementing software updates may all be considered projects. The activity of defining a standard operating procedure also can be considered a project.

Some may consider each task or activity to have a defined start and finish and could be defined as a project. Throughout O&M, there are changes made to a system. They could be routine such as updating antivirus software on a workstation, or as unique as adding a new medication as an orderable item. While these may fit the definition of a project, applying the methodology to a task or activity with a short duration would not be very efficient. Each organization identifies a threshold for projects. It may be any activity that takes more than 40 hours of effort, and more than one team, is a project. Anything less is not.

Changes made outside of projects, based on the identified threshold, should follow a change management process. This process defines how the changes will be reviewed, approved, and tracked from development through testing and put into production. Changes are typically assigned to a release where they are tested together and moved to production. This book does not go in depth on change and release management as it occurs outside of the project, but they are further discussed in Chapter 13, Transition to Support.

While there are many differences between projects and operations, there are some shared characteristics: both are performed by people, constrained by limited resources and are planned, executed, and controlled.

Program and Portfolio Management

A program is a group of interrelated projects managed in a coordinated way, or a single large project broken down into individual subprojects. Projects are managed within a program when the outcomes are dependent on each other, and it is therefore prudent to manage them together. Managing the projects together, in a single program, provides control over the predecessors, risks, and resources that managing them separately does not provide. In addition to the projects, there are program level activities that require defined processes that would be defined in a program management methodology as well as program management tools and infrastructure.

Program management is the coordinated management of a program to realize its strategic objectives. This is accomplished by integrating the cost, schedule, and effort of multiple projects. A project manager is assigned to each project to manage the day-to-day work, while the program manager focuses on the interdependencies between and across all of the associated projects.

Program managers deal with resource constraints and risks at a program level to ensure that what happens with one project does not negatively impact another or the program as a whole. The program manager coordinates the work between projects but does not manage the individual projects. The program manager is accountable for the entire program and is looking at the big picture, while the project managers focus on the details of each project, they are accountable for. They should be the first level of escalation for any project-related issues, risks, or concerns and can provide guidance and assistance to the project managers as needed.

Not all projects within the program start or end at the same time or even have the same durations. Some programs deliver benefits all at once, while others deliver the benefits incrementally. This aspect would depend on the uniqueness of the program, as well as the implementation strategy.

For a program to implement an electronic health record (EHR) with prescription drug monitoring program (PDMP) for opioid management, research protocol order sets, and advanced clinical documentation, the benefits may be realized at the end of the project. This would be if the project's implementation strategy calls for all functionality to go-live at once, referred to as a Big Bang implementation. If the implementation strategy were to bring the functionality live in phases, such as PDMP followed by the order sets, then the clinical documentation, the benefits would be realized on an incremental basis. It is the program manager who ensures that each go-live integrates with the systems, or functionality, already implemented and all interdependent activities occur as scheduled. There will be programs for which no choice on the implementation strategy is available. The program itself dictates the strategy.

A program manager must have the same skills as a project manager, such as facilitation, communication, and leadership. Program managers must also have knowledge and understanding of the organization's strategic goals and objectives, along with an ability to see the big picture across multiple projects. Having the ability to understand and communicate the organization's strategic vision, and the ability to step away from the detailed day-to-day project work, is what helps a project manager move into the program manager role.

A portfolio may be described differently across organizations. When referring to projects and programs, a portfolio is a collection of projects and programs (see Figure 2.1). Another definition for the portfolio is the management of the organization's collection of applications and systems.

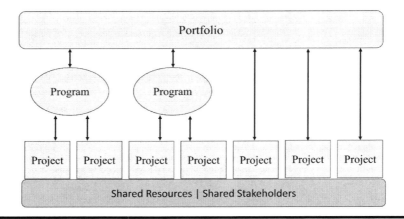

Figure 2.1   Portfolio, programs, and projects.

This would include all programs and projects, as well as all work efforts to support and maintain the systems themselves. With either definition, the ultimate goal of the portfolio is to meet strategic objectives.

The portfolio manager must be able to go beyond the management of a single project, or program, to manage all activities required to implement the systems and to keep them available for the staff to support the mission of the organization. One goal of the portfolio manager is to maximize the value of the portfolio by evaluating new projects or programs for inclusion and work with the governance committee as they make approval and priority decisions to the entire organization. This is an important step when there are competing priorities and limited resources. Ensuring resources are spent on the right IT investments increases fiscal responsibility, especially critical given the limited resource of most healthcare organizations.

As organizations realize the benefits of project management, the next logical step is to build a team of project managers. However, a team of two or more project managers with a focus on managing projects does not necessarily create a project management office (PMO). There are multiple types of PMOs, and they typically provide one or more of the following:

■ Project management standards
■ Project management guidelines
■ Education
■ Mentoring
■ Project auditing

- Project management-related software, tools, and templates
- Project management resources

The focus of a PMO is on the centralized and coordinated management of an organization's projects, programs, or the portfolio. Therefore, it may be referred to as a program management office, project management office, or a project portfolio office.

The prioritization of new project requests to ensure they are tied to overall business objectives and organizational goals may be completed by the PMO. Often, these decisions are made at a higher level, but a member of the PMO should be involved in the analysis and to provide input on the impact on which projects should be started and when. They are able to answer questions such as the following: What will it take to complete the project? Do we have the resources available for this project? Are there competing priorities with current projects underway? Answers to these questions will help leadership make a good, educated decision on new projects.

Key features and benefits a PMO may provide include the following:

- Human resources to manage projects
- Knowledge of how to complete similar projects, tasks required, duration of tasks, potential risks, and resources required
- Centralized resource for information and communication, for all projects
- A standard methodology followed for all projects
- A centralized management of project tools, such as project management software, templates, and document storage
- A centralized source for education and mentoring of project managers
- A coordinated management of overall issues, risks, and timelines across all projects within the PMO
- Assurance that all project work is aligned with the organization's strategic objectives

Project management is growing in the healthcare industry, and the concepts of program and portfolio management are becoming more widespread along with PMOs. The keys are to put the right people in the project, program, or portfolio manager roles and to have a clear methodology that is followed consistently while allowing for tailoring based on project size and complexity.

Table 2.1 Comparisons between Project, Program, and Portfolio Management

Process Group	Project	Program	Portfolio
Initiation	• Single focus with a defined set of stakeholders	• Larger focus with interrelated goals and objectives	• Organizational focus with strategic goals and objectives
Planning	• Scope with defined objectives • Progressively elaborated through project's lifecycle	• The program management plan provides guidance to the project managers on the scope and plan for the individual projects. Coordinated delivery of projects in a coordinated way	• Portfolio manager produces and maintains the processes, tools and communications for the entire portfolio of programs and projects
Execution	• Continuously update plans as more information is gathered • Project manager manages team to ensure tasks are completed according to the plans	• Program manager manages the program staff and the project managers to ensure the program level tasks are complete according to the plan • Provide guidance, vision, and overall leadership to the entire program team	• Portfolio managers manage the portfolio staff, program management staff, and possibly the project management staff • Provide strategic vision and guidance for the entire portfolio
Monitor and control	• Project managers follow defined change management processes to control the project management plan • Project managers monitor and control all work defined within project and associate risks	• Program managers follow defined change management processes to control the program management plan and work with project managers for impacts to their projects based on the approved change • Monitors the overall program's progress and risks	• Portfolio managers continuously monitor the organizational goals and objectives as they change to ensure portfolio remains aligned • Portfolio managers manage the combined resource allocation, performance, and risks within the portfolio
Closing	• Success is measured by producing expected deliverables	• Success is measured by how the overall program meets the defined needs and benefits to the organization	• Success is measured by the performance of the investment and the benefits produced by the portfolio as a whole

Case Study 1: Implementation of an Electronic Health Record

Type: Commercial off-the-shelf

Included Functionality

- Prescription drug monitoring program (PDMP) for opioid management
- Research protocol order sets, and advanced clinical documentation,
- Provide advanced clinical documentation for patient care staff

Current Situation

Your organization has an EHR system from a well-known vendor. You have been assigned to implement the additional functionality listed above, that is now available. Upon review of your current situation, you learn that the functionality is only available with the latest version of the system, therefore an upgrade will also be required.

Questions

1. Would this implementation be managed as a project or a program?
2. If managed as a program, how would you break it up into separate related projects?

Feedback

Feedback for this case study can be found in Appendix A.

Case Study 2: Implementation of a Research Tracking System

Type: Custom development

Included Functionality

- Allow online data entry as well as upload from spreadsheets
- Provide a method for the end users to query and report on the data
- Provide ability to ensure users only have access to their research data

Current Situation

You have been asked to develop software to help manage multiple research studies. This will replace the multiple spreadsheets currently in use to track the data. Upon review of the current situation, you find that there are multiple studies in progress and the researchers want to limit who has access to their data. The request for reports includes the ability for the user to query the data through a user friendly tool and produce reports ad hoc based on the queries.

Questions

1. Would this implementation be managed as a project or a program?
2. If managed as a program, how would you break it up into separate related projects?

Feedback

Feedback for this case study can be found in Appendix A.

Chapter 3

Project Process Groups

A boss says, "you do it," a leader says, "Let's do it".

Amit Kalantri

Project management is accomplished by applying knowledge and skills while using tools and standard processes to meet project objectives. A project moves through a defined set of process groups, from the initial definition of need to the final release of resources. While these process groups are well defined, it is not necessary to apply them consistently across all projects. Because all projects are unique, it is the project manager, along with the project team and sponsors, who determines how each project will move through the process groups. This is determined during project planning and is how the methodology is tailored to fit the unique project needs.

Every project can be divided into five project management process groups, as shown in Figure 3.1 and defined below.

1. Initiating—this process group defines the business need and authorizes the project.
2. Planning—this process group finalizes the project scope and the plan for how the team will accomplish the project objectives and meet the defined need.
3. Executing—this process group utilizes project resources to complete the approved project management plan that was defined in the planning process group.
4. Monitoring and controlling—this process group ensures the scheduled quality measures are completed through ongoing monitoring

DOI: 10.4324/9781003206668-3

of progress. This monitoring identifies variances to the project management plan and associated corrective actions taken to meet the project objectives.

5. Closing—this process group is where the final product, service, or result is accepted, and closure activities are completed to formally end the project.

Many of these processes are iterative throughout the project's lifecycle. The more the project manager learns about a project, the greater degree of detail there is to be managed. The process groups are not defined phases in the project's lifecycle and they often overlap as shown in Figure 3.1. It is possible to go through one or more process groups within a single project phase. Planning, for example, is never completely done, since each accepted change, risk, or issue requires some level of planning or replanning.

Most experienced project managers understand that there needs to be some flexibility within the methodology to allow it to be adapted to the individual project. Defined objectives and the complexities that come from risks, schedule, resources, and the amount of historic information further delineate a project's uniqueness. The defined activities and deliverables in each process group should be considered as guides, which project managers, with their knowledge and skill, use to determine the best way to tailor them for their specific project. There is one constant: each project flows through all process groups in one form or another.

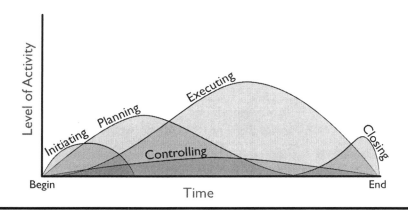

Figure 3.1   The five project management process groups.

Initiating Process Group

The initiating process group includes all activities that lead up to the formal authorization to begin the new project. These activities are often started, and sometimes even completed, prior to the project manager being assigned. This can lead to the perception that this phase has been skipped, but, in fact, an understanding of the business needs, and objectives of the project is always done, even if it is not officially documented. Following a formal process for the analysis and documentation of the different options to meet the business goals ensures that the project that is ultimately authorized will actually meet the need and fit into the organization's strategic objectives and that resources will be allocated.

All projects are approved after some form of analysis or data gathering. Determining the initial definition of need is usually the first step, followed by some level of evaluation about what will be required to meet the need. A new project request is usually in response to a problem, an opportunity, or a new business requirement. Once the initial request is identified and communicated, there should be a consistent process to follow for the evaluation of options and the relationship between the project and the organization's strategic plan. This process can be informal and may not be documented until the volume of requests causes constraints with budget and resources. At this point a business case may be requested for project justification. Some level of information is necessary for an organization to make the decision to move forward. The best decisions are educated decisions that are made after careful analysis and sound estimates are presented.

The following are possible questions to help evaluate new project requests:

- Why should we do this? What are the benefits to the organization?
- What is the final expected outcome? How does it align with the organizational goals?
- What are the risks if the project is approved? Rejected?
- What is the expected cost, and is this within the budget?
- What is the ongoing expected cost for support and maintenance? Is there room in the budget?
- What assumptions were made when developing the project request?
- What constraints will impact this project?

- What are the expected resources needed to implement this project? Are they available?
- What other options are available for meeting these objectives?

The main deliverable of the initiating process group is the project charter. At a very high level, the project charter includes a description of what is requested, justification for the request, the project objectives, a list of the final deliverables, the estimated duration, and a forecast of the resources required. Other information that may be requested includes the organizational benefit, expected cost for the project, and any ongoing support costs.

In projects with multiple phases, this process is carried out at the beginning of each phase to validate that the assumptions and decisions from the initial project charter are still accurate. An organization might choose to not require these steps, either because the project has been preauthorized or is the result of a regulatory requirement where it is mandated. This process is also repeated for agile projects as they move through multiple sprints. Agile methods are discussed further in Chapter 6.

If this is the case, the organization may not require a project charter at all. Instead, they may take the information gathered in this process group and move directly to the planning phase. While this is not best practice, it does happen. The analysis should still occur even if the formal document is not created, since this information will be used to develop the detailed project management plan.

While the project is defined at a high-level in the project charter, there should be further definition of the necessary resources needed. Human resources are often defined by what skills or types of staff are necessary for the project team. The evaluation of current staff will help identify whether these skills are available within the organization or if contract staff are necessary to supplement the project team. Other resources to be considered are new hardware, software, equipment, facilities, or supplies. Does this project include the purchase of a software package, or will the project include developing new software? Will there be any license fees that need to be included in the budget? As with most software purchases, there is typically ongoing costs for its use, which should be considered and budgeted for also.

Understanding what hardware is required for this project, such as workstations, scanners, cameras, printers, or servers, will depend on what is required and what is currently available. All of these answers feed into the estimated budget for the project but are rarely included in the initial request.

If the project manager is not already involved, he or she should be brought in at this time to work with the key stakeholders to create the project charter. While the project management office (PMO) may help with the development of the charter, the approval and funding are typically external to the PMO. The project manager works with the requestor to begin the process of identification of project stakeholders. While there are often many stakeholders for each project, there will be a few key stakeholders who will be actively involved in the project. Stakeholders are further discussed in Chapter 8. The project manager and the key stakeholders are involved during this process to ensure shared ownership, buy-in to the process, and accurate documentation of the objectives and deliverables.

The charter is reviewed during the prioritization process that defines which requests will be authorized and when they can begin. This process is usually accomplished through a governance committee or senior leadership meeting. Acceptance of the project charter provides formal approval to move forward with the project. At times, the tough decision must be made to not move forward. This might be due to resource constraints, different organizational objectives, or competing priorities. However, a project that has gone forward and is now approved moves into the planning process group once it is ready to officially begin. If a project manager still has not been identified, it is important to assign one now.

Typical contents of the project charter include the following:

- Project title
- Estimated start and finish dates
- Business need, goals, and scope
- Justification and background
- Organizational benefit
- High-level deliverables
- Project manager and authorized level of authority
- Key project stakeholders
- High-level human resources needed
- Other resources needed
- High-level milestones and estimated timeline
- High-level budget estimation
- SWOT (strengths, weaknesses, opportunities, and threats) analysis
- Assumptions and constraint
- Risks and risk management strategy
- Critical measures of success

Planning Process Group

The planning process group takes the information gathered and documented during initiation to develop the project management plan. This plan further defines the objectives and then outlines the course of action to complete the project. The information in the project charter is only one source used for the detailed planning that occurs during this phase.

Further discussion with the project stakeholders is required to gather and document their specific detailed requirements. In addition, historic documentation from other similar projects can be used as inputs for the planning processes in which the primary deliverable is the project management plan. The project management plan is actually multiple coordinated documents or plans that, combined, define the project and how it will be accomplished. Some documents are consistent across all projects, such as the risk management plan, while others, such as the schedule, are highly unique to each project.

The Project Management Plan includes the following which define the standard processes for how each will be developed, managed, and if any approvals are needed. They also include the process for managing changes that may be necessary during the project lifecycle. Depending on the organization's project management methodology, there may be project specific versions of these documents as well. These are further defined in the project planning section of this chapter.

- Scope management plan
- Requirements management plan
- Schedule management plan
- Cost management plan
- Quality management plan
- Resource management plan
- Communications management plan
- Risk management plan
- Procurement management plan
- Change management plan
- Configuration management plan

The Project Management Plan also includes the following documents which are typically unique to each project:

- Stakeholder engagement plan
- Scope baseline
- Schedule baseline
- Cost baseline
- Performance measurement baseline
- Project lifecycle description
- Development approach
- Management reviews

The project scope document is less formal and is typically shorter than the project charter. If the project has been already approved, an organization might choose to skip the project charter and only require a project scope document. The scope takes the information from the charter and further defines the boundaries of the project to include what will and will not be included, or what is in and out of scope. Defining what is out of scope can be as important as defining what is in. This will help with preventing scope creep when a decision is made to not include a specific item as part of the project.

The detailed requirements can be collected, and documented, during the project planning process group or they could be the initial step in the execution process group. There are various opinions on where this activity fits, they do help to define the scope and tasks required to complete planning, but this can be accomplished with high-level requirements. The need to create four (4) custom reports may be enough to complete planning while the detailed requirements for each report could be collected, and documented, after the standard reports can be viewed and evaluated. This may not happen until after the new system has been installed during project execution.

The project team is identified and their roles within the project are further defined. There are often many unknowns during the planning phase, so any assumptions made should also be documented in the scope. These same assumptions can often feed into any risks that might be identified during this phase. Members of the project team are the subject matter experts who help not only the project manager define the contents of the scope but also the remainder of the project management plan. The team provides the details about what activities or tasks are needed to complete the objectives, as well as how long each will take to complete. These details are used to create the work breakdown structure, which some organizations call the work plan. This is the listing tasks related to the deliverables and project work, divided into more manageable components including when each will be completed. Resources also are added to each task to define who will be needed and when. This helps the negotiation for having the project resources available when they are needed.

As the project management plan is defined, it becomes clearer what is required to complete the project. This information feeds into the final project budget that begins with the high-level budget produced in the initiation phase. The budget might include line items such as new hardware, software, travel, staff training, facility expenses, license fees, equipment, supplies, and supplemental staffing. Some organizations keep track of internal employee salary costs in the budget, while others do not; it is best to work with your finance department to understand their expectations. The project manager may or may not be actively involved in developing and managing the budget. At a minimum, they would provide input as the items are purchased, received, or completed, so the budget officer can keep the plan up to date.

One critical piece that is often overlooked is the process to define the success factors. There are two parts to this process. The first is to define how to evaluate whether the project is successful. The final evaluation of project success is done during the closing process group, even though each deliverable is tested and accepted upon completion. The project success factors, which are focused on the outcome of the actual project, must be measurable at the end of the project. The second part is to define how well the project met the business need. This may not be able to be measured at the end of the project, since the benefits are rarely obtained right away. Often, these are measured over time by analyzing trends that show improvements. These success factors should be defined during the project in the form, of a strategic metrics plan that outlines what will be measured, by whom, and when. These two concepts will be defined in Chapter 14.

While many plans are unique to each project, some should be used consistently across all projects. The risk management plan, communication management plan, and scope management plan are examples. How risks are identified and managed throughout the project should be consistent; consistency should be found as well in the use of any tools used to document the risks and risk responses.

A consistent communication management plan ensures that all stakeholders understand how communication will be managed during the project. This plan also outlines the expectations for how project manager will define, document, and monitor communications for the specific project, including any available templates. It is useful to document the who, what, when, and how the project communication will occur related to the specific project. This document would reference the communication management plan but provides more details, such as when status meetings will be held and who will be invited to attend. While the communication management plan defines the standards and expectations surrounding project communication, the details such as when communication regarding end user training or the actual activation will be unique for each project. The template mentioned previously allows for consistency of format and communication paths while allowing for uniqueness in the specific details.

A change management plan defines how any requests for changes will be managed. While this is often used to control changes to the scope, it should be used for any requested changes, especially for any project documents that have been formally approved. This would relate to documents such as requirements or workflow processes that feed into work assigned further into the project. Changes to the content of these documents will have an impact on the work being completed. For example, a change to the content of a report may have an impact to the duration of the development depending on where in the project the request is submitted. If the report development has not started yet, the impact might be minimal, but if the report is being tested already, the impact would be larger. This plan defines how these requests are managed, the analysis to be completed, and who has the authority to approve or deny the requested change. Risks, issues, and changes often feed into the iterative reviews of the project management plan.

Each project should have at least one project sponsor. This is the person who provides the direction of the project. He or she has the authority to approve the project management plan and any requested changes, assist with aspects that need escalation, and often manages the funding.

Once the project management plan is complete, and approved, the project manager schedules a kick-off meeting. The kick-off includes the project stakeholders and is held at the end of the planning process group to ensure everyone is aware of what the project is, who will be involved, and how it will be completed. This activity ensures the project stakeholders, including the project resources assigned during the planning process group, are informed of the contents of the project management plan and how they fit into the success of the project. This is often the final planning activity.

Some organizations hold a kick-off at the beginning of the planning process group during which the authorized project is reviewed, and the resources are assigned to begin planning. Neither option is wrong. The project manager would focus the content of the meeting to the project specifics known at the time and the work to be done to complete the project.

Executing Process Group

The executing process group occurs when the activities defined in the project management plan are completed. The project manager must coordinate the people and other resources to facilitate completion of the work scheduled. This process group, along with the monitoring and controlling process group, makes up the longest part (timewise) of the project, and both process groups occur concurrently.

To keep the schedule on time, the project manager must continuously monitor any competing priorities while managing the requirements. Scope time, cost, and quality must all be balanced to ensure that the project is completed on time, on budget, and delivers a quality product that meets expectations. Any change to one of these will impact one, or all, of the others.

The project manager will need to assemble the project team if they have not been brought together already. In some situations, the resources will be fully dedicated to the project, while in others, they may only have a percent of their time allocated to the project. The project manager needs to work within the available parameters to build a cohesive team. It is important to build the group of independent people, from various parts of the organization, into a team where members can trust each other and can work together.

The project manager is the primary point of contact for project information. The communication plan outlines the details surrounding the distribution of information. One method of communication with the project team is accomplished through status and ad hoc meetings from which the information is shared through meeting minutes. Working in a virtual environment adds additional challenges in building the team and with team communication. With the availability of virtual meetings, where files, desktops, and video can be shared, the project manager has more tools available for communication to team members in another building, another state, or even another country.

Providing project-specific information to project stakeholders, such as sponsors and governance committee members, is often accomplished through status reports. These are completed at regular intervals and provide a high-level account of the project at a single point in time. Communication occurs during these scheduled times, as well as throughout the project following the defined communication plan. Project communications is further defined in Chapter 8.

Monitoring and Controlling Process Group

As mentioned earlier, this process group occurs concurrent to the executing process group. Monitoring the execution of the project management plan helps to identify potential problems, and the ongoing measurement of project performance, to identify any variances to the plan. Managing changes to the project will help ensure that a change to one area is controlled, approved as needed, and integrated across the entire project. When changes are not controlled, the project manager must take corrective action to bring the project back into alignment with the project management plan. With careful monitoring, the project manager can take preventative actions to help avoid or limit any variances from occurring.

Periodic evaluation of the project performance ensures the quality of the final deliverable. There are many tools that can be used for quality reviews. These include quality audits, along with benchmarking and testing. While it is important to ensure the quality of the deliverable, it is also important to validate that the deliverable meets the requirements that were defined and approved. A deliverable that does not meet the requirements is not beneficial, even if it is of high quality. Software testing will be defined in Chapter 11.

Risks identified in the initiating or planning process groups should be continuously monitored and re-evaluated throughout the project. The defined risk response plans should be updated whenever new information is obtained. As the timeframe for a risk passes, the risk should be closed. Early identification of new risks ensures timely response planning. Monitoring the conditions that might trigger a risk allows the project manager to quickly implement the response and evaluate its effectiveness. If risk management is done correctly, it is often unnoticed, since the responses are planned and implemented quickly to resolve problems as they arise.

TIP

If risk management is done correctly, it is often unnoticed.

Scope creep, a common reason for failed projects, is caused by uncontrolled changes. Any change to the scope, or requirements, can negatively impact time and cost, as well as every other part of the project. Integrated change control is a formal process to help prevent scope creep. Each change request should be evaluated to understand how it would impact the project, as well as ensuring that it will provide a benefit. Each change should not be undertaken until it is approved.

This approval comes from the project sponsor(s) or governance committee and should be based on an impact analysis, which identifies how the request impacts the scope, budget, schedule, resources, and other projects or work within the organization. This process is performed throughout the project, from initiation through closing, whenever a change is requested.

Some projects have defined phases based on the type of work being completed. These phases are unique to the project and should not be confused with process groups. For example, phases in a software implementation might include workflow redesign, system configuration or development, testing, training, and activation. At the end of each phase, the deliverables are reviewed to ensure the project is ready to move onto the next phase. These reviews, also called Stage-gate Reviews, ensure the project moves to the next phase only when ready. This is also a good time to perform quality reviews and verify that the project is still on track to meet the scope and requirements defined by the stakeholders. Agile processes are more iterative and defined in Chapter 6. The process of how to decide the best methodology to use for an individual project is outlined in Chapter 7.

Earned value management (EVM) is a valuable tool to monitor and control the project schedule and budget. Project managers can evaluate how the project is progressing along the plan related to the schedule and budget. Comparing the estimated schedule and budget to the actual schedule and budget at a single point in time provides a clear picture of the project performance. If a project is behind schedule or over budget, the project manager can utilize the monitoring and controlling tools to help identify the cause and perform corrective action. One of the challenges of utilizing EVM is obtaining real-time data for the budget metrics, since most accounting systems are at least 30 days behind. The common EVM calculations can be found in Appendix B. While there are many different EVM metrics that can be applied to a help evaluate the project's progress, but most organizations only utilize a few.

Closing Process Group

The closing process group begins once the project deliverables have all been delivered and accepted by the project sponsor(s). For a software project, this refers to the activation, or go-live, of the software and subsequent use by the end users. Some organizations wait to begin the project closure phase until several weeks after the activation. This allows the project team to focus on supporting end users for a period of time before beginning the closing activities. Once the project work is completed, the project documentation needs to be finalized, and the sponsors formally accept the project deliverables. This formal acceptance of the product, service, or result brings the project to an orderly close.

During this process group, all documentation is updated, finalized, and archived for use as historical information for future projects. The project team members should be retained in order to finish the project documentation. The final evaluation of project success measures is also completed and documented to demonstrate whether or not the project was successful.

Other activities include the process to finalize and close any remaining contracts. This would include contracts for any products or services related to this project. The official process of closing contracts typically is completed by someone in the contracts, or procurement, office. The project manager provides input to this process by identifying all completed deliverables and working with the contract, or procurement, department.

Bringing project stakeholders together to discuss and evaluate the lessons learned from throughout the project provides a valuable retrospective review of the project. These lessons also increase understanding of what went well that should be repeated in future projects, as well as what could be done better. It is important that the group understands this is a learning opportunity and not a time to point fingers or to apply blame. Rather this exercise provides the ability to continuously learn from one project to another to improve processes. The lessons can be gathered throughout the project, at the end of each process group or phase, as well as at the end of the project.

Formal acceptance of the project is typically completed through a formal document that evaluates the original project scope, and approved changes, against what was actually delivered at the end of the project. Do they accept the final product as is and did it include all requirements defined at the beginning of the project? Once this acceptance is obtained and all documentation is completed and archived, it is time to celebrate the successful completion of the project. The celebration is the final activity before the resources are released and the project is considered complete.

All projects move through these five process groups during their lifecycle. The amount of time spent in each process group and the exact activities included are dependent on the uniqueness of the project itself. The project manager should utilize a standard methodology that allows for tailoring based on the project need. A software project also will include at least a portion of the software lifecycle, which flows from identification of requirements through to when it is turned off and no longer in use. This lifecycle is defined in Chapter 5.

Case Study 1: Implementation of an Electronic Health Record

Type: Commercial off-the-shelf

Additional Information

The vendor offers a full suite of functionality and modules for the hospital, which includes an emergency department (ED) module. Currently, the ED does order entry in the main hospital system, but the clinical documentation is still on paper.

Questions

1. What types of training might be included in the training plan for this project/program?
2. What might be some challenges faced by the project/program team?
3. What roles, or skill sets, would be required for the project/program team?

Feedback

Feedback for this case study can be found in Appendix A.

Case Study 2: Implementation of a Research Tracking System

Type: Custom development

Additional Information

There are a limited number of people, approximately 15, who will initially use the new tracking system to manage four different research protocols. It has been identified that other teams are also interested in using the system for their research. One goal identified early is for the new system to be web-based for easy access.

Questions

1. What types of training might be included in the training plan for this project/program?
2. What might be some challenges faced by the project/program team?
3. What roles, or skill sets, would be required for the project/program team?

Feedback

Feedback for this case study can be found in Appendix A.

Chapter 4

Project Knowledge Areas

Operations keep the lights on, strategy provides the light at the
end of the tunnel, but project management is the train engine that
moves the organization forward.

Joy Gumz

The Project Management Institute (PMI) identifies multiple knowledge
areas, each contain processes that are to be accomplished for effective and
successful project management. Some lead to specific project objectives,
such as scope, cost, time, and quality management. Others provide
methods to achieve the objectives, such as those related to human resource,
communication, procurement, risk, and stakeholder management. In the
current edition of *A Guide to the Project Management Body of Knowledge*
(PMBOK) Sixth Edition, published by the Project Management Institute,
some of the knowledge areas have been modified. This was done to
improve consistency as well as acknowledge that project managers tend
to monitor, manage, and facilitate instead of control processes. These
modifications have been reflected in this chapter.

The one knowledge area that is influenced by, and influences all others,
is integration management. Project managers must have knowledge and
skills in each of these areas or have specialists who provide assistance. For
example, some large projects have dedicated schedule coordinators, risk
managers, communication specialists, or procurement contract officers.

Each of the five project management process groups defined in Chapter 3
can be mapped to these management knowledge areas. Table 4.1 demonstrates
this mapping. Note these are guidelines and the project management process

DOI: 10.4324/9781003206668-4

Table 4.1   Relationship between Knowledge Areas and Process Groups

Project Integration Management

Initiating Process Group
 	
  • Develop the project charter
 	
Planning Process Group
 	
  • Develop the project management plan
 	
Executing Process Group
 	
  • Direct and manage project activities
  • Manage project knowledge
 	
Monitoring and Controlling Process Group
 	
  • Monitor and control project activities
  • Perform integrated change control
 	
Closing Process Group
 	
  • Close the project or phase

Project Scope Management

Planning Process Group
 	
  • Plan scope management
  • Collect requirements
  • Define the project scope
  • Create the WBS
 	
Monitoring and Controlling Process Group
 	
  • Validate the scope
  • Control the scope

Project Schedule Management

Planning Process Group
 	
  • Plan schedule management
  • Define the activities
  • Sequence the activities
  • Estimate the work and durations
  • Develop the schedule
 	
Monitoring and Controlling Process Group
 	
  • Control the schedule

Table 4.1 *(Continued)*

Project Cost Management
Planning Process Group
• Plan cost management • Estimate the costs • Define the budget
Monitoring and Controlling Process Group
• Control the costs
Project Quality Management
Planning Process Group
• Plan quality management
Executing Process Group
• Manage the quality
Monitoring and Controlling Process Group
• Control the quality
Project Resource Management
Planning Process Group
• Plan the resource management • Estimate resources for activities
Executing Process Group
• Acquire the resources • Develop the project team • Manage the project team
Monitoring and Controlling Process Group
• Control the resources
Project Communications Management
Planning Process Group
• Plan communications management
Executing Process Group
• Distribute information per plan • Manage the communications
Monitoring and Controlling Process Group
• Monitor the communication

Table 4.1 *(Continued)*

Project Risk Management
Planning Process Group

• Plan risk management
   • Identify initial risks
   • Perform qualitative and quantitative risk analysis
   • Develop risk responses

Executing Process Group
• Implement the risk responses
Monitoring and Controlling Process Group
• Monitor risks   • Continuous risk identification and analysis
Project Procurement Management
Planning Process Group
• Plan procurement management
Executing Process Group
• Conduct procurements—including solicitation and source selection
Monitoring and Controlling Process Group
• Control contracts
Project Stakeholder Management
Initiating Process Group
• Identify stakeholders   • Complete initial stakeholder analysis
Planning Process Group
• Plan stakeholder engagement
Executing Process Group
• Manage stakeholder engagement & expectations
Monitoring and Controlling Process Group
• Monitor stakeholder engagement
Closing Process Group
• Final acceptance of project

should be tailored to fit the unique situation related to organizational culture, current methodology, or project management process. Chapter 5 provides an overview of software development lifecycles and different methods of managing projects and Chapter 6 reviews the different Agile methods.

Integration Management

Integration management is used in project management to coordinate activities that occur across all of the process groups and knowledge areas. The ability to look beyond any single activity or decision to see how it will impact the rest of the project is necessary to keep the work on track. Monitoring and controlling project performance and the ability to be flexible when a decision or risk may impact multiple aspects of the project are important parts of integration management.

The main activities that occur during knowledge area involve the development and management of the project management plan. This is a clear, concise plan for how the project will be completed, which begins with the project charter. The contents of the project management plan are listed in Chapter 3. The management of activities included in the plan ensures they are executed as scheduled. Controlling all project changes involves managing all changes across the entire project. This would include changes introduced by stakeholder requests, risks, issues, or changes in the organization's strategic objectives that might impact the project.

TIP

Changes will happen and should be expected.

A new activity added to this knowledge area is managing project knowledge. This new activity is related to ongoing learning throughout the project. Gathering lessons learned is no longer something that is done at the end of the project. These should be gathered throughout the project and the team should implement any necessary process change to continuously improve during the project.

Someone must focus on the big picture and take responsibility for the overall coordination of the project, and this becomes a top function of project managers who must also be able to keep their focus on multiple fronts at the same time. They need to have one eye on the day-to-day activities to ensure their timely completion, while keeping the other eye on the bigger picture to manage and control the overall project. This leads some people to feel that integration management is the key to overall project success.

Scope Management

Proper scope definition and management does not guarantee a successful project, but studies show that determining the project boundaries in the early stages is one of the main reasons for project failure. Defining scope is a difficult activity, especially when many people are providing input. Project stakeholders must come to consensus about what will and will not be included in the scope. Once defined and approved, it is the project manager's role to ensure that the entire team has the same understanding of the scope and how the final outcomes will be delivered.

TIP

The project scope should define the project deliverables and the work required to produce them. It is also important to include both what is in and out of scope to clarify the project's boundaries.

The main processes in the scope management knowledge area start with the project scope statement, within the project charter, and are elaborated with the definition and documentation of project functional requirements. The project's functional requirements define the "what" is needed in the project. However, these requirements are often gathered from stakeholders who frequently provide the how rather than the what. It takes a unique skill to obtain the true requirements from the project stakeholders, who, in many cases, often are not sure what they want.

When purchasing a commercial off-the-shelf (COTS) system from a vendor, the requirements are often gathered and documented as part of the procurement process. With this example, the requirements are frequently related to what functionality will be implemented, how the functionality will be configured or work to be completed beyond the system, such as developing integration with other systems.

If the project involves developing custom software, the requirements are often obtained during planning at least at a high-level. These requirements are usually a two-step process. The business requirements are provided by the stakeholders which define what they want the new system to do. These are analyzed to produce design and/or system requirements, which define the details about how the system will be developed to meet the business requirements.

Clear and well-defined requirements are as important as a clear and well-defined scope; without either, the end product may not meet the business need or the stakeholder's expectations. Once requirements are collected and documented and a detailed description of the project is obtained, the WBS is developed. There are now a wide range of optional frameworks for managing this type of project. Each have their own characteristics, pros, and cons. Chapter 5 discusses the software development lifecycle in more depth and Chapter 6 provides an overview of Agile methods.

The WBS provides a structured view of the project as the deliverables are broken down into smaller, manageable components. The smallest components are called work packages, and these can be used to estimate the schedule. Utilizing expert judgment as well as historical documentation from previous similar projects, the WBS leads to the scope baseline and develops the project schedule. As an organization, or project manager, tailors the methodology for managing their project, the traditional WBS may not be used. The project manager may only utilize a task list, or workplan. This is a typical process for smaller projects.

Scope change control involves controlling changes to the project scope. Each change request should be analyzed to determine the impact it will have on the project, as well as on any other projects in the organization's portfolio. Once the impact analysis is complete, an educated decision is made to accept or reject the change. The key is not to prevent changes but rather ensure the impact is known before a decision is made. Change management does not only refer to the scope. Changes to requirements, once approved, can have the same impact on the project, even if the changes do not impact the scope directly.

Schedule Management

Completing a project on time is one of the main measures of success, but also one of the biggest challenges. Issues with the schedule tend to cause the most conflicts across the project lifecycle. Once a project schedule is set and communicated, it is often the most common measurement of project performance. Once project stakeholders are given an end date, the expectation will be set, and it is sometimes difficult to reset even with approved scope changes that impact the schedule. These approved changes should be taken into account when comparing planned activity times with actual activity times when determined if a project is on time.

TIP

Be careful when communicating project activation or end dates, because they may change during long projects. Instead, provide stakeholders an approximate date range. As the project progresses, you can refine and specify actual dates as the schedule is further refined.

Project schedule management involves all activities related to completing the project. While this sounds simple, it is far from easy and it all begins with proper planning. The project manager works with the subject matter experts (SMEs) within the project team to identify the tasks necessary to complete the scope and project deliverables. This identification activity includes defining the expected work effort, duration, cost, resource requirements, and sequence of each task. Obtaining the actual activities, or tasks, from the SMEs can sometimes be as much of an art form as obtaining requirements from stakeholders. As these are defined, the relationships between activities must be understood to ensure proper sequencing.

With most healthcare organizations, the project resources are not dedicated to one specific project, so the difference between work effort and duration can be challenging to define. Often, the resources are also supporting other systems and may even be working on multiple projects. This provides challenges to controlling the schedule when an issue with a current production system arises and is a higher priority than the planned project work.

When implementing a COTS system, the vendor can assist with the activity definition, based on their past experiences with other clients. They often know what activities are necessary and what detailed tasks are needed to complete them. Defining these activities, when developing new software, is not as straightforward. The development model utilized will impact the activities involved. Will a prototype be developed? Will they develop and deliver the software in phases or through an agile process? Software development is a more iterative process, during which a portion of the development is completed and shown to the customer who provides feedback. This feedback is reviewed, and more development is completed, then shown to the customer again. This process tends to add some complexity to developing and controlling the schedule. How many iterations will be included? If requirements were not documented well or the customer is not sure of what they want, this can go on for many cycles, making it difficult to identify the end of the project. This is often the difference between selecting a system where you can see the functionality and how it works vs. trying to define what you want without being able to see functionality and its process up front.

Once the schedule is complete and approved, it must be controlled, as with any other portion of the project. Any change to the project can affect the schedule, although it is important to note that not all changes will increase the timeline; some may reduce the duration, especially requested changes based on the need to complete the project sooner.

Cost Management

Information technology (IT) projects can be expensive and even balloon way over budget. If you are unable to obtain good requirements or good estimations of activities, the project budget will be difficult to get right. Most IT projects include new technology or new business processes. If these are untested, their use can lead to risks that cause increased costs, whereas well-defined projects, using proven technology and accurate time estimates, can lead to realistic budgets. Depending on the amount of risk and confidence in the schedule, the budget could include an amount of money set aside as part of the contingency plan.

When purchasing a COTS system from a vendor, the quote usually includes only the costs from that vendor. This will often include software licenses, services to assist with implementation, and possibly hardware, depending on the vendor and contract. This is often what is used to start the budget. The organization should consider if they will include internal costs, such as the organization's resources that will be working on the project. Depending on the project, the budget may need to include additional items. Will this project utilize currently owned hardware or software, in addition to what is purchased from the vendor, or will new servers or third-party software be required? What other human resources will be needed such as contracted supplemental staff? Depending on when the project manager is assigned to the project, the budget and contract could already be defined and in place.

The costs for software development tend to be more variable. The reliability of the requirements will feed into the reliability of the budget. There is a higher risk, in software development, of having an extended project timeline. This is due to the multiple iterations and that it is difficult to estimate how many will be required before the project deliverables meet the customer's needs or expectations. There can also be a learning curve if new technology is utilized for development. On top of these considerations, there remain some of the same issues as already discussed, even if the development work is done within the organization or through a contract with another company. A good project manager needs to understand basic cost management concepts to help control the budget. This relates to organizations in which the project budget is managed by the project manager or managed elsewhere, such as through the finance department.

Quality Management

As quality can be defined so many different ways, it is important to understand how the stakeholders define quality related to this particular project. Some see quality as the final outcome being in compliance with the project's requirements. Others focus on how well the final product meets the intended use or improves their workflow. Conformance to requirements and fitness for use are only two ways to define quality. The primary purpose of quality management is to ensure that the final product meets the business need. Some measures of quality are evaluated during the project, while others cannot be calculated for months after the project ends. It is important to remember that the customer decides if the quality of the final product is acceptable.

The quality planning process includes identifying the quality standards that are related to this specific project, how they will be met, and how they will be measured. For IT projects, this might relate to response time, accuracy of the data, or the amount of time the system is available, or uptime. This process evaluates the project performance based on the quality standards defined in the quality management plan. There are many tools and techniques available to help manage and control quality where results are measured through inspections of deliverables based on metrics defined and approved in the quality management plan.

TIP

- Quality planning defines how quality will be measured.
- Quality control is the actual act of validation or testing.
- Quality assurance is the evaluation of the quality process in relation to the project.

One important technique to measure quality for IT projects is often through the validation phase in the project's lifecycle. Most testing occurs after the development of a software component or at the completion of all development. The different types of testing are defined in Chapter 11. Testing can validate all requirements are met, that the performance meets expectations, and/or how well the system fits with the redesigned workflow. There is also a validation step that occurs during the activation. Testing resources includes the actual developers, testers, and even the end users. All have a role in proper testing prior to activation or go-live.

The plan should also include how to measure quality outside of the project. How well the deliverables meet the business need cannot always be measured prior to the project ending. Some metrics require 6, 12, or even 18 months of using the final product prior to obtaining meaningful metrics. This is because there is often a period of time where the users are still learning the new system, or the new workflow. Efficiencies are hard to measure during this learning time. The measures of success are further discussed in Chapter 14.

Resource Management

Project resource management is a vital skill for all project managers. This knowledge area goes beyond just human resources, or the team, to include all resources required for the project. The team may consist of people who have not worked together before, and it is the project manager's job to form them into a team to complete the project. High-level resource needs are identified in the project charter and the needs are further refined during the planning phase. Taking this information and further estimating the resources needed for the project occurs in the planning process group, but also reviewed and updated throughout the project. The project manager is often accountable for identifying, acquiring, and controlling all project resources.

The process to acquiring the necessary skills for the project team varies depending on the organization. Negotiating for the staff's time to work on the project, when they are needed, can be challenging especially when there are competing priorities. During this process, the project roles and responsibilities are defined.

Once the team is assigned, team development should occur when necessary. Even the most talented individuals must learn to work as a team to achieve the project's goals. To be effective, they need to be able to utilize their individual strengths while working with others that they may or may not know. Training for the project team on the new software or technology should also be identified during the planning phase and is often required prior to or at the beginning of the execution phase.

The project manager will need to work closely with the team member's human resource manager, unless the organization has a project organizational structure wherein the team reports directly to the project manager. This collaboration helps with prioritizing competing work and any conflicts among the team members. The project manager should have the opportunity to provide input into the team member's performance reviews. In this situation, the project manager has the authority to direct staff's work, but only within the project. During closing, the release of resources allows the team members to move on to other activities or projects.

Communication Management

Communication is more than just obtaining and distributing information. It involves understanding the information received and being able to explain it to others. It is well known that IT professionals have their own language with terminology that is not often understood by outsiders. This is also true with the healthcare industry. There needs to be someone on the team who can understand both sides and help translate as needed. Informatics, a healthcare discipline that continues to grow, blends information science, computer science, and healthcare science. The ability to help with communication is just one benefit that informatics can bring to the project team.

When the stakeholders are identified, the project manager should understand how each would contribute to the project. This analysis feeds into the communication plan, ensuring that the right information is shared with the right people at the right time using the right communication vehicle and the right terminology. Even though the project manager is often the hub of the project communication, distributing information, such as the status of tasks, newly identified risks, or issues and their resolution, is part of every team member's responsibility. The reporting of project performance includes regular status reports to stakeholders, governance committees, and project team members. These are often snap shots in time communicating how the project is progressing with what activities have been completed and what is scheduled for the next time period. They also include new risks and issues that need to be escalated. This communication helps manage stakeholder expectations and should include the information they ask for based on their interest in the project.

The communication plan defines the who, what, when, where, and how of all project communication and helps to set expectations related to the sharing of project information. The needs and expectations of the stakeholders are taken into consideration when developing this plan. As the project progresses, the plan may require modifications or revisions. An approved scope change may lead to the identification of new stakeholders requiring communication and collaboration. Stakeholder management and communication planning is further discussed in Chapter 8.

During the closing phase, the project manager must ensure that all project documentation is complete and archived. Team members should not be released until this activity is complete. The administrative closure documentation is completed by the project manager and involves formal acceptance of the project by the stakeholders. All project documentation becomes historical information for future projects.

Risk Management

Risk management is the process of identifying, analyzing, and responding to risks throughout the project. Early identification of risks is the responsibility of all project team members. This is critical, as the earlier risks are identified, the more time there is to perform risk analysis and plan the risk response. Communication of risks to stakeholders helps them understand the nature of the project and helps with managing their expectations. Proper risk management is a form of insurance to lessen the impact of potential adverse events. This is the area in which most organizations can improve their project performance.

Many organizations struggle with a balance between risk and opportunity. The opportunity that comes from a new system must be weighed against the risks. Different organizations have different risk tolerances. Do you want to be on the leading edge of technology, willing to take additional risk to be the first to implement and use the new solution? Your organization would be a risk-seeker.

At the other end of the spectrum are the risk-adverse, who have a lower tolerance for risk and want to play it safe. A risk-adverse organization prefers to implement technology after it has been proven stable and reliable. The middle ground is risk-neutral, the point at which the organization seeks a balance between risk and benefit.

Risk analysis looks to evaluate each risk to estimate the probability of occurrence and the impact to the project. Quantifying risks helps the project manager prioritize them to determine the threshold for which risks deserve the most attention. Ones with a higher probability of occurrence with a higher impact to the project should be carefully monitored. Involving members of the project team, SMEs such as security and privacy resources, will help with the understanding of the risk and how best to manage its response.

After the analysis, the organization must decide on a response for each. Eliminating the risk, often by removing the cause, is an example of risk avoidance. This requires a change to the project to remove the cause of the risk, such as eliminating a deliverable, modifying the requirement, or changing a member of the project team. Risk acceptance occurs when the organization accepts the consequences if the risk occurs because they either cannot do anything to avoid it or the impact is minimal. When a risk is accepted, a contingency plan should be developed, and funds set aside to support the contingency plan.

Reducing the impact or probability of the risk event is a method of risk mitigation; if the impact is high enough, the project manager may attempt to do both. Any risk mitigation activities should be added to the project schedule.

Risk management continues throughout the project by monitoring the identified risks and implementing the risk response when needed. As the project progresses, new risks can be identified and will require analysis. Some risks may be closed before the project ends. For example, the risk that the hardware will not arrive on time can be closed after the hardware is delivered and verified to be what was ordered.

Procurement Management

Procurement is a term used by organizations to describe obtaining goods or services from an outside source. Others may use terms such as *purchasing, contracting,* or *outsourcing.* In these organizations, procurement management may also be called purchasing management, contract management, or outsourcing management. It is important to understand that this process includes more than just managing contracts. It also includes planning, proposal development, proposal response evaluation, and negotiation, through management of the awarded contract and proper contract closure.

Organizations purchase software from vendors, such as a surgical system, a pharmacy system, or a full electronic health record system. Outsourcing is usually used to acquire temporary resources to supplement the in-house staff on a project when the necessary skill set is not available; for example, a healthcare organization may not have developers on staff to build custom software. While these purchases need to be managed and controlled during the project, most organizations have specific departments for this work. The project manager works in collaboration with this team to review deliverables and compare them to the contract.

Procurement planning involves determining what to purchase. The first step includes defining what the requirements are for the purchase. If it is unclear what is available, a market analysis, or market research, can be conducted. This process can lead a make-or-buy decision. If there isn't a vendor that can meet the organization's requirements, it might decide to build rather than buy.

Solicitation planning includes the development of a request for proposal (RFP). This document includes full requirements to ensure that the selected vendor can meet them. Source selection occurs after each RFP response is evaluated and the contract is negotiated. Each organization has their own processes for who is involved in these activities, as well as what occurs at each step. The process also differs between the public and private sectors. The need to be objective and unbiased is required for anyone participating in procurement management.

Sometimes, the vendor's staff is brought in to work beside the organization's staff on the project team. Managing the relationship with the vendor is part of managing the project team. Who manages the contract is dependent upon the organization. The project manager is the person who confirms that the activities are completed, and milestones are met on schedule that leads to contract payments. During the closing phase, all contracted deliverables are confirmed, and all open items are resolved. Once formal acceptance is completed, the contract is closed out. The administrative process for contract closeout has been moved to the Integration management knowledge area.

Project Stakeholder Management

Stakeholder management begins by identifying the people or groups that are impacted by, or may impact, the project. This includes the project team, the sponsors, end users, and even the vendors involved. The identification of stakeholders begins in the initiating process group and continues throughout the project. Once the stakeholders are identified, an analysis of their impact to the project and expectations should occur. Stakeholders and the stakeholder analysis are further discussed in Chapter 8. Throughout the project lifecycle, the project manager should monitor and manage the stakeholder engagement. This relates to the commitment and communication of each stakeholder throughout the project.

Case Study 1: Implementation of an Electronic Health Record

Type: COTS

Additional Information

The vendor provides a standard WBS work plan that outlines a 16-month implementation plan. The new hardware has been ordered. They have assigned the following resources:

■ Project manager: to manage vendor work and resources
■ Trainer: to provide training for project team and super users
■ Clinical consultant: to facilitate workflow redesign
■ Configuration consultant: to provide guidance and assistance for system build and customization
■ Technical specialist: to provide guidance and assistance for the technical configuration related to hardware and database
■ Technical interface specialist: to provide guidance and assistance for the interface development

Questions

1. What types of requirements are needed for this project/program?
2. What types of line items would you expect to find on the budget?
3. Who would you expect to be stakeholders for this project/program?
4. What methods of communication might the project manager utilize for this project/program?

Feedback

Feedback for this case study can be found in Appendix A.

Case Study 2: Implementation of an Organizational Metrics Dashboard

Type: Custom development

Additional Information

The project sponsor has identified key people with whom the team should work to define requirements. They will be the super users who can also assist with testing. An experienced developer from the IT department will develop the new system. He will develop the software using a development platform/technology he has used in the past and it can be hosted on current servers in the data center.

Questions

1. What types of requirements are needed for this project/program?
2. What types of line items would you expect to find on the budget?
3. Who would you expect to be stakeholders for this project/program?
4. What methods of communication might the project manager utilize for this project/program?

Feedback

Feedback for this case study can be found in Appendix A.

Chapter 5

Software Development Lifecycle

> It is amazing what you can accomplish if you do not care who gets
> the credit.
>
> **Harry S. Truman**

All software has a specific lifecycle. It begins with the initial identification of
a need and ends when it is no longer needed and is disposed. The details of
the lifecycle will vary amongst applications and the management processes
in place. This chapter will provide an overview of the software development
lifecycle (SDLC) which has specific phases that all will go through at one
time or another. There is no single model that is correct or that fits all
applications.

There have been, and still are, multiple different versions of the SDLC.
They may have different names for the phases, may move from one to
the other in a linear fashion, or repeat them in an iterative manor. But the
phases themselves are fairly standard.

The standard phases of the SDLC are:

- Requirements
- Analysis, or specification
- Design
- Configuration, construction, or development
- Validation, or testing
- Installation, or deployment

DOI: 10.4324/9781003206668-5

- Operations and maintenance, or support
- Retirement, or disposition

TIP

All software moves through these phases even if each follows a different path.

The project manager may only be involved at specific times during a software's lifecycle. They will get involved once the initial project is approved and ready to begin. They may also be involved for projects that arise during operations and maintenance such as upgrades or adding new functionality. If an iterative process is followed, a project manager may be involved for a longer period of time. These are phases of the software's lifecycle, not a project's lifecycle.

As mentioned above, there are various methods available for managing the SDLC. If a linear method is followed, the application will move through this one phase at a time. If a more iterative method is used, these phases will be revisited with each iteration. Once the software is initially implemented and moves to operations and maintenance, they previous phases may be revisited in a new project, even if a linear method is followed. This will be discussed further below.

The process begins with a request or identification of a need. This can be considered the first requirements, even if they are vague and non-specific. The need must be met for the project to be successful. How detailed the requirements will be, and when they are collected, will depend on the methodology being used. Early stakeholder involvement when defining the project scope and system requirements helps to build ownership in the process and the final product. But stakeholder involvement is not enough to ensure that the requirements are accurately captured. A strong business or systems analyst has the skills to facilitate the identification of the requirements and documentation to the level expected by the project team. The iterative models provide the stakeholders with the ability to review and refine their requirements through the incremental process. This allows them time to better understand what they need and want prior to getting to the concise and complete requirements.

Requirements can be gathered and documented in different ways. Business requirements provide a description of what functionality being requested. These are called user stories in Agile methods. These are analyzed to determine the best way to meet them. After the analysis, the technical requirements, or system design, are determined. These outline how the system will be developed to meet the business requirements. Iterative methods may repeat this process for each cycle, or sprint. This process may include screen layouts, business rules, process diagrams, architecture designs, or mock-ups of any reports or outputs. The level of documentation and use of stakeholder review meetings will vary based on the methodology. However, the requirements are defined and documented, they feed into the testing phase to ensure all aspects of the software is validated.

Walkthroughs are used to review documentation, such as the specifications or design. The documents are sent out to the walkthrough team prior to the meeting, so they can be reviewed individually. During the walkthrough meeting, the areas that require clarification or are identified as incorrect are discussed. The process can be done by each person reviewing his or her notes or by going through the document from start to finish, with the team providing input throughout. The latter tends to be more comprehensive. The focus of walkthroughs is to identify incorrect items, so they can be brought back to the appropriate team member to resolve.

A process that is similar to walkthroughs but is more formal is an inspection. This process involves inspecting the design, or the actual development code, and looking for any errors. An overview of the item being inspected is provided prior to distributing for review. During the inspection meeting, each item is covered at least once to ensure full review. As with walkthroughs, the focus is on identifying errors, not to correct them. A written report is produced listing all errors found, which is provided to the appropriate staff for rework. When all items are resolved, there is follow-up to ensure that all corrections are checked. Walkthroughs and inspections are not included in all methodologies, at least not as formal meetings.

Once all requirements and designs are approved, the development begins. This includes actually programming the code that is the base for the system. The developer often completes unit testing during this phase. Any requested changes to the requirements are completed through a formal change management process and are completed only after approval. If one of the iterative models is used, prototypes will be shown to the stakeholders at key points in the development process. In Agile methods, these would be the product at the end of the sprint. This validation step allows for feedback on what was developed. Since the iterative models, including Agile, embrace and allow for change, there is no formal change management process requiring approvals.

TIP

The product lifecycle lasts the entire life of the product, from initial concept, through retirement, but the project lifecycle only lasts as long as it takes to produce the approved deliverables.

The system is tested at various stages through the lifecycle, depending on the SDLC model and the project management plan. As mentioned earlier, unit testing occurs during development and further testing follows. If a prototype is accepted, functional testing may follow while other development proceeds or may wait for all development to be completed. For an iterative method, testing would occur prior to each release. The test plan is defined during the planning phase of the project and outlines exactly what types of testing will be included and when each will occur. The testing includes validation of the final product against the requirements, as well as verifying the quality of the system against any bugs or issues. The different types of testing, which are part of the quality control process, are defined in Chapter 11.

Testing is followed by stakeholder acceptance and deployment or activation. The stakeholders should accept the system prior to it being deployed into a production environment and the end users begin using it. This is often accomplished through a series of go/no-go meetings during which the system's operational readiness is reviewed. These reviews include the status of any last-minute activities, outstanding issues, or bugs, as well as any go/no-go criteria defined earlier in the project. During this time, planning is occurring for the activation, or go-live. This activity is often forgotten until the very end and there is little time left for planning. Management of the activation activities is defined in Chapter 12.

Once the system is live, it needs to be transitioned to operations and maintenance. Who will support the software once in use? What is the process for end users to request modifications or report issues? System changes should follow a standard change and release management process to ensure that only approved changes are made and the proper documentation and testing occur prior to migrating it to the production system. Transition to support is further discussed in Chapter 13.

During the operations and maintenance phase, there may be additional projects that are needed. These maybe for software or hardware upgrades, new integration with other systems or additional functionality. While the application does not officially go back to the beginning of the lifecycle during these projects, some activities from each phase will be necessary per the project management methodology. The software is still in the operations and maintenance phase of its lifecycle, which is the longest phase.

At some point, the organization will determine that the software is no longer necessary. Either it no longer meets the needs of the stakeholders, or it is being replaced by another system. At this time, the software would move into the last phase, disposition. This is where the organization needs to decide what to do with the data in the system, the software itself, and the associated hardware. Wherever possible, these should be destroyed per the security and privacy policies. If the data needs to be kept, it can be migrated to a new system or saved in an acceptable location for access. If the system needs to be retained to access the data, it is not ready for disposition.

Waterfall Model

The Waterfall Model is the original SDLC model. Each phase is clearly defined and must be completed prior to moving on to the next. This starts with gathering the requirements, which are verified by the stakeholders or a group identified by the stakeholders. The specification phase is the documentation of the functionality required within the system. Once the specification document is approved, the project management plan for development is defined. Once the stakeholders approve the project management plan, the design phase begins.

During the design phase, if something is unclear or incomplete, the work stops, and the project moves back to the specification phase in a feedback loop until the specifications and design are verified. The implementation phase also includes a feedback loop that allows for modifications to be made to the requirements, specification document, or even the design document, as necessary. Modules are developed, implemented, tested, and then integrated with each other to form the complete system.

The vast majority of a system budget is spent on operations and maintenance, from implementation through to retirement. Proper planning for this phase is necessary, and the disciplined approach continues well after the initial development is over. This model does include full documentation and stakeholder approval before moving on to the next phase.

The advantages of the Waterfall Model include a disciplined approach that is enforced through the required documentation and verification for each phase. The milestone ending each phase is the verification of all deliverables, including documentation, by the stakeholders or their designees. Testing and validation are inherent to each phase, so this activity occurs throughout the process and not in its own phase after development. This emphasis on documentation can be a disadvantage if the stakeholders are verifying and approving documents that they do not understand or don't take the time to read thoroughly.

Spiral Model

The Spiral Model is a modified version of the Waterfall designed to decrease the risks surrounding software development by the use of prototypes and risk analysis. Some consider this to be the first iterative process. Each phase begins with an analysis of the risks at that time. Each significant risk should be resolved before proceeding to the next phase. The use of prototypes alone helps reduce risks. With each prototype representing specific functionality, the verification of project durations and requirements are more easily measured. Each cycle of the spiral depicts a phase of this iterative development lifecycle, with prototypes developed at different phases. The focus on multiple prototypes minimizes scope creep and focuses the work effort on management project pieces.

There are many advantages to the Spiral Model. The emphasis on risk analysis and prototypes provides validation that the project is on schedule and meeting requirements. Maintenance is another cycle in the spiral, so this is treated the same as the initial development. This model lends itself to large-scale development projects. This is because the cost of multiple risk analyses can overshadow some smaller projects that may have much smaller budgets.

Rapid Prototype Model

This model begins with a rapid prototype, or working model, of a portion of the final system. The rapid prototype should be developed quickly to speed up the development process. This is provided to the stakeholders or end users to experiment with and utilize to verify that it meets their needs. Once the real requirements are verified, the prototype is often discarded. This phase is followed with phases similar to the Waterfall Model with specification, design, implementation, and integration prior to operations and retirement. This model provides rapid validation of requirements but can extend the length of development over the traditional Waterfall Model.

Incremental Model

The Incremental Model builds software during each of the steps. Each step, or increment, goes through the same processes until the final system is complete. The initial phases are similar to the other models, starting with requirements, specification, and design. Each incremental build goes through detailed design, implementation, integration, testing, and delivery to the end users. These phases are repeated over and over again until all pieces are delivered, and all requirements are met.

During planning, the number and content of the incremental builds are determined. They should be significant enough to provide sufficient new functionality to avoid spending an exceptional amount of time with regression testing for the benefits provided. This model provides a functioning system at the end of each incremental build but with only a portion of the functionality requested. This allows the end users to begin using the system earlier than with the other models but only a portion of what they need at a time and each incremental build needs to be integrated with the previous versions. This does allow the ability to terminate the development at any time with some benefit delivered.

Agile Development

Agile software development allows for requirements and deliverables to evolve through a collaborative approach. This allows for adaptive planning and early deliverables and encourages rapid and flexible responses to change. With this model, working software is delivered frequently, in weeks rather than months. The work is broken up into small increments, which decreases the upfront planning and design. Each of these iterations, also called sprints, lasts from one to four weeks and involves a cross-functional team working in all functions, such as planning, analysis, design, development, unit testing, and acceptance testing. At the end of each sprint, the deliverable is shared with the stakeholders.

In this model, communication and collaboration are very important. The stakeholders need to be available to answer questions, review the deliverables, and provide input throughout the project. There are daily meetings where the team members provide a status of their work, identify any roadblocks, and discuss the next steps. Agile development uses an adaptive method with specific milestones defined while allowing flexibility in how to reach them. The Spiral, Rapid Prototype, and Incremental models are, in some respects, all agile with iterative approaches and they have laid the path for what is now called Agile development. Agile is discussed further in Chapter 6.

Commercial Off-the-Shelf (COTS)

When purchasing a COTS system, the vendor has already gone through the initial phases of the development lifecycle. The requirements were gathered from subject matter experts, who are employed by the vendor, are contractors, or work for organizations partnering with the vendor. The system is in the operations phase and is available for purchase. These types of systems are not custom developed for one specific need, rather they have been developed to meet a general purpose within the marketplace. These are systems that can be used within the emergency department, radiology department, a physician's practice, or throughout the organization, such as an electronic health record. They can also be smaller niche systems, such as for nurse scheduling or physician credentialing. These systems are typically delivered with basic functionality and with the capability for the customer to utilize defined tools to customize them for their unique needs and workflows.

Implementing a COTS system follows a similar lifecycle. Understanding the business need is always the first step. Since the implementation begins with the purchase of the system, the beginning is usually focused on the procurement, or purchasing, process. This process can vary between organizations, public and private sectors, or when there is a previous agreement with the vendor such as adding a new module to a current system. The activity of gathering and understanding the requirements is necessary early in the process for market research, which determines if there is anything on the market to meet the need. This helps with the decision to buy or build. This process typically occurs during the project initiation process.

Once a new system has been purchased, the project planning begins. The vendor should provide resources to assist with the implementation of the system and provides guidance on what activities they consider as standard, based on past experience with other clients. During this phase, the organization should make a decision about what functionality will be implemented and when. The project scope should identify whether all available functionalities will be implemented as part of the project or not. If not, which features will be will be implemented should be clearly documented in the project scope. The implementation plan should also include the activation strategy. Will this system go live all at once, as a Big Bang? Will it go live in phases, one module, or section of the organization at a time?

During planning, it is important to remember that workflows will change and enough time needs to be scheduled for process redesign activities. When documenting the current workflows, remember that documented processes or procedures do not always match what really happens. The real workflows need to be documented to understand how they might change when the new system is implemented. This is similar to the requirements and design phase of the SDLC.

When moving to any form of automation, the workflows will often change more than moving from one system to another. Benefits and efficiencies are not realized when workflows are automated as they are with manual practices; there should be some improvement provided by the new system. Representatives of end-users must be involved in the process redesign activities to ensure that the future workflows will fit into their daily work. The documented future workflows feed into testing scenarios, as well as training materials, and provide guidance for post-live support.

The vendor can assist with defining the activities surrounding the configuration of the system. This phase is similar to the build or development phase of the SDLC. Most systems on the market allow for some configuration based on the unique organizational processes. The more customization allowed, the better the system will fit within the organization's processes, but also, the longer this phase will last. These can be simple items such as defining the format for the date and time, or they can be more complex such as configuring structured notes for clinical documentation.

The contract with the vendor should define who would be assigned to do these activities. Will the vendor do all configuration based on decisions made by the organization, or will they provide training and guidance to allow the organization's information technology or clinical staff to complete these activities? Either way, the project manager and contracting officer should manage the contract to ensure that everything is delivered and completed as defined.

All systems go through an SDLC from initial identification of need through disposition. The organization is actively involved in this process for custom-developed software that is built for their specific needs. When the organization purchases a new system to fill the need, the system has already gone through most of the development lifecycle. There is still a need to go through similar phases to identify and complete the customization prior to testing and activation. Custom developed software may follow an Agile process for the lifecycle which is further defined in Chapter 6.

Case Study 1: Implementation of an Electronic Health Record

Type: COTS

Additional Information

The vendor has provided details about how the new system can be customized. The organization can decide and build the following:

- Order sets that can be used for Opioid medications or research protocols
- Alerts based on recent Opioid orders for the patient
- Format used for clinical documentation
- How clinical documentation is displayed once entered
- Reports to be displayed and printed from the system

Question

1. What phases would this project/program include?

Feedback

Feedback for this case study can be found in Appendix A.

Case Study 2: Implementation of an Organizational Metrics Dashboard

Type: Custom development

Additional Information

The following functionality is being requested:

- Allow direct data entry for four independent research studies.
- Provide the ability to load the past two years' worth of data
- Provide dashboard views of data with the ability to click on any value to view more details.

Question

1. What phases would this project/program include?

Feedback

Feedback for this case study can be found in Appendix A.

Chapter 6

Agile Development Methodology

Intelligence is the ability to adapt to change.

Stephen Hawking

Agile is not a methodology, but rather it is a set of principles and values. The need for an alternative to the documentation focused and linear path for software development processes led to the emergence of the Agile Manifesto.[1] This effort produced a new way to develop software that was thought to be better than the traditional waterfall method. The new mindset was built on several values that focuses on individuals, software that actually works, collaboration with the customers, and being able to respond to change. As Agile spread, project teams were using the new approach in many situations beyond just software development.

It became clear that a broad range of tools, techniques, and frameworks were needed to achieve successful projects. The development of a new common language and mindset was needed as this was very different than the traditional waterfall methodology as it allowed for flexibility. The outcome provided new choices on how to manage software projects. This chapter will introduce the terminology, concepts, and a few of the different methods that make up Agile software development.

DOI: 10.4324/9781003206668-6

The Agile Mindset

The main purpose of development is to create. While tools and processes are important, having good people working together, collaboratively and effectively, is the main focus of the Agile mindset. The belief is that the interactions are more important than the tools or the processes. Software development requires working closely with the customers, allowing for, and accepting, changes as the combined team works to discover what is actually needed. There is the belief that working software is more important than comprehensive system documentation. The term Agile means being able to move easily and quickly and applying that to software development removes the rigid constraints of linear processes such as waterfall. Every method and framework that follows these values can be called Agile.

While the agile movement is not necessarily anti-methodology, it allows for a more balanced process between the documentation that is needed and the need for documentation. Below are the 12 principles of agile software development based on the Agile Manifesto.[2]

1. Our highest priority is to satisfy the customer through early and continuous delivery of valuable software.
2. Welcome changing requirements, even late in development. Agile processes harness change for the customer's competitive advantage.
3. Deliver working software frequently, from a couple of weeks to a couple of months, with a preference to the shorter timescale.
4. Business people and developers must work together daily throughout the project.
5. Build projects around motivated individuals. Give them the environment and support they need and trust them to get the job done.
6. The most efficient and effective method of conveying information to and within a development team is face-to-face conversation.
7. Working software is the primary measure of progress.
8. Agile processes promote sustainable development. The sponsors, developers, and users should be able to maintain a constant pace indefinitely.
9. Continuous attention to technical excellence and good design enhances agility.
10. Simplicity—the art of maximizing the amount of work not done—is essential.

11. The best architectures, requirements, and designs emerge from self-organizing teams.
12. At regular intervals, the team reflects on how to become more effective, then tunes and adjusts its behavior accordingly.

Agile Methods

The key values and principles listed above apply to all agile methods, but there are a variety of distinct methodologies within the Agile world. The top Agile methods and frameworks by developers are listed below. While they all follow the same basic principles, there are some differences.

Scrum Framework is a lightweight process that is a subset of Agile. It allows teams to respond efficiently, effectively, and rapidly to change. Scrum provides the structure to generate organizational value through an adaptive solution. Key components of Scrum are roles, artifacts, and time boxes, also called sprints. The team is small and includes specific roles. The core roles include a scrum master who is accountable for and leads the Scrum team, a product owner who is accountable to managing the product backlog, and the developers. The main artifacts used in Scrum include the product backlog, sprint backlog, and the released product. The product backlog is the list of all items to be developed for the product, the sprint backlog are the items assigned to the specific sprint, and the released product is all functionalities made available in a release which typically includes the items from multiple sprints. The development is completed in an iterative fashion through short sprints. The scrum framework is often confused with Agile, but while Agile is a set of principles and a mindset for managing projects, Scrum is one of the most popular frameworks used to put Agile into practice.

Lean is focused on improving processes and it originated in manufacturing. The principles are to build quality into the product while eliminating waste and delivering it fast. The waste that is typically eliminated include unnecessary meetings, documentation, or tasks that do not provide value to the quality output. Some believe Agile, and many of the different methods, are decedents from Lean thinking that has been applied to software development.

The **Kaban** method emerged in the mid-2000s and is less strict than some of the other Agile approaches. It can be applied easily at any point in the project and is a good predecessor to the other agile methods if the organization chooses to move in that direction. A key principle here is to focus on reducing the time from start to finish with continuous flow rather than defined sprints. Another unique feature of this method is the Kaban board which provides a visualization of the work and helps the team improve the workflow. The board has discreate items written on a card that is moved around the board as it progresses through the different stages of development. This can be done manually with a physical board or digitally with an electronic tool.

Extreme Programming (XP) utilizes an engineering process to produce a higher quality software in a more productive manner. It delivers software that is needed, when it is needed, and empowers developers to respond to changing requirements. XP is often thought of as the most radical of all Agile methods. Managers, customers, and developers are all equal members of the collaborative team with strong communication, a key element. Customers emphasize the most useful features thought testimonials and the developers base each successive software upgrade on this feedback. Creativity is encouraged by the developers and mistakes are a natural part of the process.

There are many additional Agile methods available and more are identified as teams determine there is a need to modify a current framework to meet new needs. Some additional methods that are common include Crystal, Dynamic Systems Development Method (DSDM), and Feature Driven Development (FDD). The remainder of this chapter will focus on providing an overview of the commonalities of the Agile methods.

Life Cycle Selection

As each project is unique, the project management approach will be unique and needs to match the project. There are four basic types of life cycles that will be described in this section, plus the hybrid approach which is further defined in Chapter 7.

The **Predictive** life cycle is the more traditional approach with most of the planning completed up front, followed by execution in a sequential way. The most common form of this life cycle is the Waterfall approach. These approaches assume there are firm requirements and low risk. There is a detailed plan providing the team with the knowledge of what to deliver, how, and when. Business value is delivered at the end of the project.

The **Iterative** life cycle permits feedback on unfinished work, allowing for modification and improvement. This life cycle utilizes prototypes or proof-of-concepts to improve the product or result. Each iterative version allows for stakeholder feedback, which is then incorporated into the next cycle. The iterations help to identify and reduce uncertainty in the project. This is beneficial when the project is highly complex, there is no consensus on the scope, or there are frequent changes. Iterative life cycles are optimized for learning, not speed of delivery, so the duration tends to be longer.

The **Incremental** life cycle provides completed functionality that the customer can utilize right away, but in smaller deliverables. The team plans for the output prior to starting any work and begin the development of the first deliverable right away. Because of the rapid delivery of incremental products, the team can manage changes to requirements or even the original vision for the scope.

The **Agile** life cycle is both iterative and incremental providing an approach that refines work and delivers frequently. The development team expects change, and the combination of iterative and incremental approaches allows for improved planning for the next part of the project.

Hybrid Life Cycle is where elements of different approaches are combined to achieve the specific goals of the unique project. Most healthcare organizations are using a hybrid approach, not an exact version of any single life cycle. They may have a strong influence of one while including some pieces of the other. Chapter 7 provides guidance on choosing the right project management method for a specific project.

TIP

Many organizations tend to adopt a hybrid approach that mixes elements of Agile software development with other approaches.

Common Agile Practices and Terms

Retrospectives allow for the team to learn, improve, and adapt the process. These fit with the Agile Manifesto and the principle of having the team reflect on how to improve at regular intervals and adjusting the behavior based on what is learned. Many teams include the retrospective at the end of each iteration, but it could be completed at any milestone during the project. A facilitator leads the team through this activity and helps them rank the importance of each finding and when they should be applied for continuous improvement.

A **User Story** is a brief explanation of a feature, or functionality, written in the viewpoint of the user. These are the format that requirements are documented in Agile methods. The user story is the smallest level of work to be defined and are assigned to specific sprints.

An **Epic** is a larger user story that is bigger in scope and covers more substantial amounts of functionality. These may be broken down into multiple related user stories before being assigned for development.

The **Backlog** is a list of all the work, presented in the form of user stories or epics. The product owner, with input from the team, produces a product roadmap that shows the anticipated order of development over time. The roadmap is refined as the project progresses through each iteration and subsequent reviews. During the refinement meetings, the stories are reviewed, and any potential problems or challenges are identified.

Sprints are a short, time-boxed, period where the team completes a set of work, or delivery cycle. The sprint includes all work required to produce a deliverable product based on one or more user stories. These are typically two to four weeks in length and include the development of all the assigned functionality or features.

A **Release** is when the product is delivered to the users and typically includes the outputs of multiple sprints. Each release is planned and includes migrating the code through the different environments, testing, training, and communicating as one package. This is not unlike the release management process for ongoing operations and maintenance.

Daily Standups are short meetings that occur daily to review the task board, obtain status updates, and uncover any problems. Topics include what was done yesterday and what is to be accomplished today. The goal is to keep these meetings to less than 15 minutes.

Demonstrations and **reviews** are where the working product is shared with the product owner at the end of an iteration or on a set schedule. Feedback is gathered during these meetings to keep the developers on track and identify where modifications are needed.

A **Burndown Chart** is a visual representation of the work remaining within the time left in the spring. In contrast, the **Burnup Chart** is a visual representation of the work completed toward the product release.

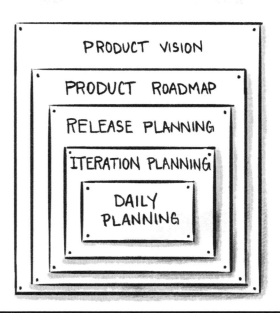

Figure 6.1   The levels of Agile planning.

There are multiple levels of planning in Agile methods (see Figure 6.1). Product vision provides the overall definition for the final product. The roadmap provides guidance on how the team will reach the final product. There is also planning that occurs at the sprint level, called iteration planning, and at the release level. Daily scrum meetings help to communicate the plan for each day.

Agile methods are focused on the principles of satisfying customers, improving interactions, and collaboration. Having software that works as expected is how progress is measured and the team should be able to continuously reflect and adapt. Some organizations believe pure Agile practices are inefficient or too extreme for their culture. These organizations tend to adopt a hybrid approach that mixes elements of Agile software development with other approaches. Others feel Agile is not a project management methodology at all, rather a product management methodology. Projects have a characteristic of a defined beginning and end. With Agile, and the ability to adopt to changes quickly, it may be difficult to define an actual project end. The process can be an ongoing cycle that continues until there are no further requests for modification or change. This characteristic of Agile processes is what leads to the product management viewpoint.

Notes

1. History: The Agile Manifesto, accessed January 31, 2021, https://agilemanifesto.org/history.html.
2. 12 Principles Behind the Agile Manifesto. (2019, October 06). Retrieved January 31, 2021, from https://www.agilealliance.org/agile101/12-principles-behind-the-agile-manifesto/.

Chapter 7

Choosing the Right Methodology

Judy Wight

> Whenever you are given two choices, look out for the third option.
>
> **Sara Arinto**

When a project manager is assigned a new project, one of the first choices is to decide the strategic execution plan to accomplish the work. Thankfully, there is an ever-expanding universe of project management methodologies and frameworks to choose from. Selecting the "right" one will have a profound and ongoing impact on the project's success or failure.

What does "Methodology" Mean?

No two projects are the same and one size does not fit all—some methods are geared for speed and improvisation, while others are built for predictability and comprehensiveness. Either way, the project manager should tailor the methodology to accommodate the unique qualities of the individual project. The project manager will need to deliberately adapt the execution plan to the business, stakeholders, the industry, organizational culture, organizational maturity, project phase, resources and skills, etc.

Project management methodologies provide a blueprint of how to deliver projects. They are an approach to "doing something." Some execution strategies demonstrate a well thought-out, defined, repeatable approach, prescribing the "what to do" and "how to do it." They come with a defined

DOI: 10.4324/9781003206668-7

set of rules, techniques, activities, deliverables, and processes to solve a specific problem. For example, a fast food restaurant that must deliver consistent meals for its customers will need to follow a well-defined methodology so that staff do not ever have wonder what and how to deliver the food.

Other methodologies are looser. They also provide structure and direction about a preferred way to do work; however, they are not as detailed or rigid. Guidelines, rather than prescriptive rules, describe what to do. They rely on the doer to determine the best way to get the "what" done. These types of methodologies are flexible enough to adapt to changing conditions or to be customized, allowing for a great deal of room on how the project manager applies components of the framework. For example, this type of method would better suit a master chef in a gourmet restaurant, where only the desired outcome is known. Given a well-equipped kitchen and a stocked pantry, the chef can produce an outstanding meal without being told how to prepare it.

For the purposes of this discussion, a methodology refers to principles, practices, procedures, techniques, and rules that the project manager and team apply to guide the process of achieving project goals. The primary methodologies covered include Waterfall, Agile, and Hybrid models.

Why Is Choosing a Methodology Important?

Project management is important to organizations and teams, but for it to be effective, the project management methodology must match the team type, project, organization, and goals. Choosing the right methodology or framework for running a project matters because it defines how the project manager and team will accomplish the work. You cannot use a hammer to open a screw, after all. Indeed, a core reason behind project failures is due to selecting the wrong project management methodology.

Some projects are straightforward and predictable, while others are complex and risky. Applying the same amount of project management rigor—regardless of the need—to every project may end up being wasteful. To make an informed decision for the business, the project manager must develop the knowledge and skills needed to apply multiple project management methodologies and must also choose the approach that lies somewhere between over-relying on a methodology and rejecting all project management.

The best methodology is one that allows the project manager and the team to deliver a solution in a way that optimizes the team's time, guides work toward meeting strategic objectives with the greatest gains and least negative impact and maximizes end user satisfaction. A pragmatic, rather than dogmatic, approach makes sense when choosing a methodology. Project teams are also learning to combine the different styles, discovering new benefits and succeeding at delivering projects.

Characteristics of Each Methodology

Briefly, this chapter will cover the major characteristics of Waterfall, Agile, and Hybrid methodologies, including advantages and disadvantages. This chapter does not provide a definitive guide on these methodologies, as those topics could (and do) fill many books. Instead, the section provides an overview to assist in deciding what makes the most sense for a project or organization.

Waterfall

Waterfall refers to a methodology that adheres to the philosophy of "do it once and do it right the first time." This well-known strategy follows a linear, sequential approach along a single, long lifecycle with multiple stages. Progress cascades downward in one direction—like a waterfall.

The project manager and stakeholders define requirements and expectations extensively and in detail from the beginning, before any work starts. Once authorities approve the project scope and execution begins, it follows a specific sequence of phases, adhering to the defined requirements and following a linear direction. Change requests and further approvals are required to modify the scope, schedule, or budget once the plan is approved.

Each stage is self-contained and completed before the next phase can begin. The outcome of one phase acts as the input for the next phase in a sequential pattern. As such, once a phase has completed, it is not revisited. Stakeholders are involved only during milestone check-ins and delivery time and budget are fixed. In Waterfall, project management processes are clearly defined and keeping complete and consistent documentation is paramount. Finally, given the extensive early planning, the project manager plays a large role in Waterfall.

Pros

Waterfall is well-known, straightforward, and is easy to understand, implement, and use. Investing time in the early stages of a project ensures design and requirements are identified and documented up front, so expectations are set from the beginning. The stages are intuitive and easy to grasp, regardless of prior experience. The structure provides a clear differentiation between stages that helps to organize and divide the work into chunks. Making sure the product is "perfect" at the end of each stage often leads to better results in the final product. Gathering, understanding, and documenting requirements make it easier for new resources to get up to speed and work on the project when needed. Plans from previous projects can be copied and applied to new project with minor adjustments.

This logical, methodical process works well for manufacturing and construction industries because they are creating physical products and follow linear assembly lines. For example, when you are building nuclear waste disposal system, executing a series of well thought out steps, and meeting hard deadlines to deliver a complete project that satisfies all defined requirements is what you want—every feature better be near perfect before it is put into production! In addition, Waterfall works well for projects include implementing commercial off-the-shelf (COTS) software and performing simple upgrades or releases to an existing application, etc.

Cons

This simple methodology has some obvious disadvantages. Waterfall assumes that the project manager, sponsor, and stakeholders have a deep understanding of the requirements and that these will be correctly identified and analyzed at the beginning of the project. This methodology follows a heavily structured process and if an error is found along the way in requirements or there is a need to change something after a stage is complete, the project must restart from the beginning of the last stage (or earlier). This circumstance potentially increases risks and costs and may push out the timeline.

Another criticism of Waterfall is that its main purpose is to help internal teams move more efficiently rather than focusing on the end user or customer. Stakeholders are not given the opportunity to provide input during development, except at formal Stage Gates, when milestones are reached, at User Acceptance Testing, or when the product is released. In addition, saving the testing phase until the later stages of a project is risky, as this leaves room for problems to remain unnoticed until the project has neared completion. In either of these cases, major revisions could cause significant delays or cost more to develop.

Agile

Agile is more of a philosophy, ideology, or approach with development based on specific values and principles. The actual execution method comes in many flavors, such as Scrum Methodology, Lean Software Development, Kanban, Extreme Programming (XP), Crystal, Dynamic Systems Development Method (DSDM), Feature Driven Development (FDD), etc. Each of these Agile methods brings their own set of characteristics, terminology, and processes. Like Waterfall, project teams' cycle through a series of planning, executing, and evaluating. However, Agile applies a collaborative, evolving design and build process to work. Project team members execute a series of tasks and activities that are conceived, performed, and adapted as the situation demands, rather than using a pre-defined process. Self-directed, cross-functional Agile teams work in short time-boxed "sprints" to complete specific work and make it ready for review. Each of these sprints is organized into small, short deliverable units of work (also known as releases) with regular testing, feedback, and adaptation throughout the time period.

With Agile Scrum, for example, teams self-organize and are deeply collaborative. Development of the project outcome evolves, based on direct and frequent customer feedback, rather than following pre-defined phases. There is a product owner that—with input from the project team—identifies, organizes, and prioritizes items (requirements) in a list (product or sprint backlog). Team members (aka "developers") work only on those items that provide the highest value to the customer during the sprint period. At the beginning of each sprint, the Product Owner chooses the product backlog items to build in the next sprint based on the value they deliver to the customer. Minimal up-front planning is required, and it allows the team to get the ball rolling, knowing that they can adjust along the way.

The project team is always open to change if that is going to lead to an improved product. There is an assumption that project variables are unpredictable and flexibility to changing requirements are expected and welcome. Product owners, rather than project managers, play the larger role in identifying priorities and driving the project forward.

Pros

Agile methods provide fast and flexible results because the technique allows for making small incremental changes that respond to changing circumstances. Given that there is no need for heavy up-front requirements planning or fixed stages, Agile works well with short turnaround times and tight deadlines. Stakeholders provide constant feedback and Agile teams have the freedom to experiment and make iterative changes based on current customer priorities. This collaboration focuses on providing value to the customer and reduces the risk of project failure since the stakeholders are involved every step of the way.

If the project scope is only loosely defined, such as in ventures seeking to develop new, innovative, or creative products and features, the stakeholders may not know all the requirements in advance. Agile provides a method for bringing such a project to life. Even when it's unclear at the outset what the solution will look like, agile methodologies allow for adding features, services, and functionality at any point throughout the project lifecycle.

Cons

Agile methodology is sometimes praised for "not being Waterfall" and may be pitched as a means for "doing more, with less, faster and cheaper than ever before"; but this methodology does not necessarily work well for managing every type of project. With the Agile approach, there is no fixed plan. This can make scheduling and resource management exceedingly difficult as staff may be constantly brought on or taken off the project on an ad-hoc basis. One of the deficits for Agile is that because circumstances change quickly, documentation is usually limited, making it difficult for new team members to get up to speed.

Also, Agile is also prone to scope creep, unpredictable timelines, and increasing costs. With this feedback-heavy method, stakeholders must work closely with the project team—this means that product owners and project sponsors must be willing and available to offer feedback quickly and often; at the same time, stakeholder overinvolvement can lead to micromanagement that leads to loss of freedom.

For enterprise-wide solutions, organizations may opt to implement commercial-off-the-shelf (COTs) software that offers either no customization or only low or no code configuration options. In this type of project, the focus will be on gathering requirements rather than on developing code to build it. As such, resorting to a more traditional waterfall approach to design, testing, and deployment may be a better fit.

Hybrid

The Hybrid approach is sometimes referred to as "hybrid agile," "structured agile," "iterative waterfall," Agilfall," or "WAgile." Whatever the name, for some projects, neither methodology in their pure form makes sense and organizations may benefit from using an amalgam of both. Hybrid project management combines the traditional waterfall style with the more flexible Agile methods to create a new project management method. A mixed model might make sense if:

■ The organization is transitioning to a new methodology and selected practices can be rolled out over time rather than all at once.
■ Different teams that participate in the same project may want to use different methodologies.
■ Regulation or contractual requirements may require a more predictable project management approach for some part of the project; but the project team can accomplish a part of the development work using Agile.

Given the potential variables of the Business, Stakeholders, Customers and Resources and Project Characteristics and the multiple Agile strategies, there are many ways to select practices à la carte and design and implement a hybrid methodology. One such common arrangement is where the project manager uses Waterfall methods to create a high-level project roadmap and then employs Agile techniques to develop, refine, and release components and sub-components of the product. This example follows a process using the following format:

■ Gather and document all requirements
■ Obtain overall design approval
■ Perform development Iterations (sprints)
   – Design
   – Development
   – Test

- – Gather feedback on what's been produced thus far (identify changes or additions that fall within the outlined requirements based on priorities)
- – Implement changes based on that feedback and develop, test, and prompt for further input
■ Deploy to production once stakeholders are satisfied with the product

The Project Manager, Product Manager, and Team members share responsibility for different aspects of the project. The team collects requirements up front and the work is then split into small manageable chunks of work or sprints. Within each sprint, the team follows the agile sequence of design, development, testing, obtaining and integrating feedback, and then releasing. The team can deliver other sections of the project (such as acquisitions, training, etc.), if needed, using the Waterfall model. By incorporating sprints, this Hybrid approach provides flexibility to incorporate requirement changes and still deliver products on a schedule.

Pros

The advantage of a hybrid approach, such as the one described above, is that the project manager and team can define the deliverable and understand the high-level tasks and their dependencies up front, using a structured work breakdown structure. Then, the team uses Agile to speed up development and delivery of the final product using iterations. The hybrid approach has the potential to improve product quality and reduce development time.

A hybrid approach can make the planning and project estimation more accurate while providing the ability to react to changes based on demands. And once the team is past the initial planning stage, the Hybrid method affords increased flexibility when compared to the pure Waterfall method. By borrowing the initial planning phase from Waterfall, the Hybrid method addresses one of the biggest complaints about Agile—the lack of predictability.

Cons

Implementing a Hybrid approach requires that the team and stakeholders both have Waterfall and Agile expertise and experience (which is not necessarily common). The project manager, product owner, and team will need a broad range of knowledge covering both methodologies and to be good both at defining project scope and schedule while also delivering frequent and timely value.

Another disadvantage is that the team is not committing fully to either methodology and there is an overwhelming number of combinations to choose from. Organizations may in fact be maintaining the traditional mentality that hampers the Agile development. Project leadership will need to make compromises on and balance both control and flexibility. For example, from the waterfall viewpoint, the team gives up a level of certainty to gain Agile's flexibility. Inversely, agile developers lose freedom and are more limited, but the project overall gains better budget, resource, and schedule control.

Since project leadership is a shared responsibility in Hybrid methods, coordination, and communication may become muddled. For example, while overall project responsibility may be given to a Project Manager (who uses Waterfall methodology), the Scrum Masters manage sprints. The project manager may (or may not) assume the role of the Product Manager. Product Managers focus on strategy, product design, market analysis, requirements, and customer feedback rather than managing schedule, budget, and resources. The whole team needs to collaborate continuously with ongoing reporting, analysis, and reviews.

What Factors Should the Project Manager Consider in Choosing a Methodology?

An assessment of the project environment is the foundation for choosing a comprehensive execution plan. There is no right or wrong methodology—the best one is the one that fits the project, organization, and stakeholders and increases the chance of success. If the project manager misreads the environment or the methodology chosen does not address critical issues, the recovery costs can be high, resulting in project failure. The project environment includes all the conditions that could potentially influence the outcome. In making this choice, the project manager should identify, assess, and evaluate variables that impact all projects, such as the state of the Business, Stakeholders, Customers, Resources and Project Characteristics (e.g., scope, budget, timeline, constraints, tools, assumptions, etc.).

After reviewing these variables, the project manager must weigh them against the overall goals of the project and decide which method is most relevant. Compare and contrast the pros and cons of each methodology against project needs. Ask the project team and leadership which one will bring the most success and efficiency and conversely, which will bring the most risk? Finally, don't forget to monitor progress along the way and adjust as needed.

The Business

How the organization is structured, and its culture and history will impact the choice of project management methodologies. The project manager should identify and asses enterprise environmental factors, especially if a conscientious and sophisticated approach is needed. Some methodologies work well for large organizations with established hierarchies and others are more suitable for smaller, leaner companies. Each of these factors may influence the strategy chosen and adaptations to a methodology.

This is not a definitive list, but the project manager should identify, list, and evaluate the following criteria when appraising the business:

- Organization: what are objectives and goals of the organization? For example, an organizational value might be to provide exceptional customer experience or to release high-quality innovative products. This variable covers areas that executive management feels are important for continued organizational growth and development, etc. What is the organizational size and maturity level? What is the final goal of the project as it relates to strategic objectives? What organizational decision-making processes are in place and how formal are those processes? Given the experiences, ways of thinking, beliefs, and future expectations of the organization, how will the project manager navigate the political climate?
- Industry: in what business field does the organization operate, e.g., construction, information technology, manufacturing, healthcare, government agency, etc.? How fast are products launching or changing? In some industries, such as software development, the business landscape is fast changing, requiring flexibility to take advantage of new understandings and meanings or new business opportunities. If

the latest product feature is already out of date, there won't be time for a structured project management approach. In other industries, such as construction, the industry may be changing more slowly, is controlled and highly regulated, and it is extremely expensive to change anything after a structure is built.

■ Culture: what does the organization value (e.g., vision/philosophy)? In this case, culture refers to the way employees and leaders behave within the organization. Organizational culture is made up of shared beliefs and values that corporate leaders establish, communicate, and reinforce. The culture shapes employee perceptions, behaviors, and understanding and sets the context for everything an enterprise does. What is the risk tolerance of the organization? A risk adverse culture may not be willing to adopt the looser agile approach.

■ Resources: what competencies are available within the organization? Are external resources, such as freelancers and contractors, a possibility or a necessity? (Also see Stakeholders, Customers, and Resources, below).

■ Legal: what broad legal issues might impact the project including different levels of government (e.g., national, regional, local, international), security issues (e.g., local law enforcement), staff hiring and management (e.g., union or not), etc.?

■ Flexibility: what is the rigidity or flexibility of the work environment (e.g., is there a structured hierarchy with strict approval processes in place or is there a certain comfort level with uncertainty)?

■ Discipline: the existence, or absence of, a Project Management Office can have a significant impact on the use and tailoring of any project management methodology. What, if any, methodology is currently in use in the organization? If there is a PMO, is there a set standard? Are there any learnings or outcomes from previous projects that could be considered?

Stakeholders, Customers, and Resources

All projects have stakeholders. Especially in the beginning of a project, the project manager should gather information from key stakeholders and end users to determine their expectations, needs, and wants. The more well understand the stakeholders are, the more effectively the project manager can engage and influence them. Engaging stakeholders early and often enables the project manager to uncover customer attitudes, the degree of their flexibility, their desire for involvement, and their expertise to form the basis of an effective project management strategy.

Customer, stakeholder, and team thinking style is a significant factor in determining if Agile is a good fit or not. Agile methodology works well for independent thinkers who enjoy being "outside the box" and are comfortable operating apart from standard procedures. If stakeholders and team members are risk-averse, resistant to changing procedures, need concrete guidance, and/or think in linear, sequential terms, it may not work as well.

This is not a definitive list, but consider the following criteria to when evaluating stakeholders:

- How many people will be involved? How many stakeholders are there?
- What are the attitudes of project stakeholders and customers? Do the stakeholders prefer a particular methodology?
- Are the stakeholders external or internal?
- What do stakeholder expect as a project outcome? What do they expect from the project manager in terms of their needs, goals, objectives, and assumptions?
- Do the stakeholders know exactly what they want (and it isn't going to change)? Are the goals clear and unchanging from the beginning? Or do the stakeholders have only a vague idea of what they want?
- Are stakeholders known to change project scope frequently?
- Does the project cross organizational boundaries? If so, the associated challenges and considerations for the project sponsor, the project manager, and the project team increase proportionately.
- Do executive stakeholders have a strong need to be stay informed throughout the life of the project or are they more hands-off? How involved do the stakeholders want or need to be in the project? How much should the stakeholders be involved to improve chances of success?
- What is the appetite for change? Are stakeholders open to any possibility of risk?
- What do the stakeholders require from the project manager? Are stakeholders self-organizing or do they require a structure and strong leadership?
- Are stakeholders willing and able to engage frequently to give feedback?

Resources refer to the staff involved and materials or supplies that a project manager needs to execute, manage, and deliver a project. Material resources include items such as supplies, assets, or goods, such as software, licenses, hardware, infrastructure, equipment or machinery, property, testing or laboratory equipment, etc. The project manager should identify, list, and assess the tangible, intangible and human resources available to use (or are needed) to complete the project, including (but not limited to) the following:

- Procurement: are material resources needed for the project available or must they be purchased? If the organization is purchasing tangible resources for the project, what and how are they being acquired? What are the processes needed to obtain products, services, and results from outside the project team and organization?
- Project team: people who have habits, opinions, and values are the ones that carry out a project methodology. The project will, by necessity, need to involve people with the right experience, knowledge, and skills to accomplish the assigned tasks. If the project team is not capable of delivering the project using a preferred approach, it does not make sense to choose it, unless you are willing to train staff. What is the expertise level and what are the strengths and weaknesses of team members? Is the project team familiar with the project management methodology of choice or will they require training? Beyond training, will the organization need to supplement the project team with contractor staff that already have the skills needed? Will required team members be available when you need them? Is the project team solid and self-organizing? Or is it more sprawling, with a need for greater coordination? Does the team thrive on collaboration, and are they highly motivated and disciplined? Are staff remote or on-site and how might that impact communication and team dynamics?
- Project manager: what is the project manager's role in the organization and what is their sphere of influence and control? Does the project manager have the skills and knowledge needed to execute the preferred methodology? Will the organization need to allot time for the project manager to learn new techniques or will the organization need to hire already skilled Agile practitioners? Will team members or the project manager resist changes in methodology?

Project Characteristics

By definition, all projects are unique; however, there are certain common attributes—such as the traditional constraints of scope, budget, quality, and schedule, for example—that allow the project manager to develop a basic project profile. To develop an understanding of the individual project, the project manager should identify, describe, and assess the project scope, budget, and schedule, along with other factors, to determine the best execution strategy, by asking the following types of questions:

■ Scope: how well-known are the scope and deliverables? Are the project results vague and unknown or clear and well-understood? What are the required benefits of the final deliverable? What is the project size? Is the environment changing quickly, where requirements and project boundaries are difficult to define in advance? The greater the confusion around project goals and objectives, the greater the complexity and need for improvisation. Also, a project might be considered "small," but it may add tremendous value to meeting business strategic goals.

■ Budget: what is the budget for the project? What are the financial constraints? Is there room for the budget to grow if necessary, or is it essential that it stays within predetermined limits? What are the financial constraints around national, local, or industry-specific regulations that could impact the budget?

■ Timeline: how much time has been allotted to deliver the project? How long is the project expected to last? Does it have a short or long duration? Is a quick turnaround expected, or is it more important to have a perfectly finished product, no matter how long it takes? Will there be compressed schedules or is there an imposed deadline? Is the project time-sensitive (e.g., fast-tracked to get a product on the market for a conference or is the project related to monthly program events, minor software releases, advertising campaigns, etc.)?

Consider other criteria related to the project itself including (but not limited to) the following:

■ Complexity: how multifaceted is the project? Assess whether the project involves a heterogeneous and irregularly maintained system, if there are multiple interacting components, and if components interact with each other. What impact do these changes have in each phase and to the project as a whole? Ordered systems, such as an interstate toll booth or a production line in a factory, are not likely to be complex systems because they are homogenous and/or redundant and independent actions do not interact or impact each other. In addition, projects involving COTS implementations, upgrades to existing systems, and refreshing hardware/software are straight-forward and may not benefit from taking an Agile approach the way a software development effort would.

■ Product Life Cycle: all products have a life span. The product life cycle characterizes the evolution of a product, including initiation, growth, maturity, and declining stages. At what stage is the product is in its life cycle (e.g., just an idea, partially deployed, a mature product, at an end stage, etc.)? How will the project phases and hand-offs work together? What milestones, documents, processes, and other elements occur at different stages and how do they interact? A product in its operations and maintenance stage (or maturity) where the features are well defined and must interface with known or existing products, does not require a great deal of flexibility.

■ Risks and constraints: is this a large project with a big impact that needs to be carefully managed to deliver major strategic products? Or is it a smaller-scale project with a bit more room for flexibility in schedule and budget? Is the purpose of the project one of the following?
  – Respond to increased demand
  – Develop a new product line or services for future growth
  – A need for operational efficiency
  – New governmental laws or complying with new regulations and policies

If so, a more flexible approach may be necessary. Is there room for the scope and requirements to change during the process? How would changes made during different project phases impact the chance of success? Is there a rigorous stage gate process in place? If so, the organization may be risk-averse and would not welcome the potential for additional costs.

■ Tools: project management tools are often designed to work well with a specific methodology. Do the software tools and capabilities available support the requirements for a specific project management methodology?

Table 7.1 can be used as a quick reference guide to help decide on a project management methodology.

Discussion/Conclusion

Choosing an efficient and effective methodology that caters to the needs of the project can make the difference between success and failure. Be careful to choose a project management methodology that is realistic and

Table 7.1   Project Management Methodologies

Methodology	Pros	Cons	When to Use
Waterfall	• Provides a well-defined set of processes to deliver stable, predictable outcomes and deliverables within a constrained budget, and timeline. • Provides departmentalization and control, allowing teams to focus exclusively on each aspect of a stage.	• Waterfall requires heavy upfront project planning (which customers often do not want to pay for). • Adjusting to changes requires re-work that may be difficult and expensive. If unexpected requirements or a variation in the plan arises, it may require starting again from the beginning, wasting effort and time in the process.	This methodology makes more sense If: • The project includes fixed, unmovable requirements, timeline, and budget and the requirements and scope are well understood. • The project requires internal or external reviews and approvals and/or must follow strict processes. • The product owner that does not want to be hands-on and only wants milestone updates. • The project involves an enhancement to a legacy product where the features are well defined and must interface with known or existing products.

Agile	• Provides a flexible approach with enough guidance to achieve quick results without rigid rules or procedures. • Allows for project creativity and for discovery of the project's features and requirements in an iterative way. • Stakeholders may change their mind continually throughout the project.	• Flexibility can be expensive in terms of defects in the process, inconsistent outcomes, and uncertain timeframe and funds. Sometimes a new, valuable feature will be discovered, but it will require more time and money to deliver. • To be successful stakeholders must be available on an ongoing basis to provide continuous feedback on the scope and the functionality of the product and must be empowered to make decisions. • This methodology requires maturity from the stakeholders (e.g. Product Owners, customers) to understand that the product they'll get and when it will be delivered cannot be exactly defined.	This methodology makes sense if: • The project is complex, prioritizes features and speed to market, requires immediate action and these qualities are more important than documentation and process. • The organization has a high tolerance for risk and fewer processes and procedures. • The project product includes new, innovative, or creative deliverables with many unknowns, requirements that are in flux or evolving. • The stakeholders are unsure at the onset what needs to be built or they wish to discover what should be built based on adjustments they make along the way. • The stakeholders want to be deeply involved to take advantage of opportunities as the project unfolds. The product owners have an appetite for evolution and change.

(Continued)

Table 7.1   (*Continued*)

Methodology	Pros	Cons	When to Use
Hybrid	• Reasonably Flexible • Borrows from both methodologies to reduce the disadvantages of both—it includes structural elements from Waterfall to give a solid backbone to the project while allowing for changing requirements and the flexibility of Agile.	• Jack of All Trades, Master of None • Requires expertise in multiple methodologies • Roles, responsibilities, and team communication must be well defined.	This methodology makes sense if: • There is a defined end goal in mind, but the stakeholders also need flexibility. • The project is large-scale, has a large team, and/or has specific a budget or timeline and needs a nonstandard solution (e.g., requirements are not well understood).

will improve the chances of success. It might be a good time to consider whether the organization should remain as rigid or flexible as it is. Does the requestor need the product now, or do they need it better? If the project goal is to get the first version out right away, and quality can be sacrificed for the sake of innovation, Agile might work better. But if quality matters more, a more traditional Waterfall approach might be the better choice. Or, some a blended, customized approach might push the organization in the direction it needs to go.

Case Study 1: Implementation of an Electronic Health Record

Type: Commercial-off-the-shelf

Additional Information

Given that this is COTs software that will impact many employees, you are trying to decide which project management methodology makes sense. As a newly minted project manager, you that see that business users understand their requirements and there is some urgency around moving from paper-based documentation to the new EHR functionality; however, they are generally too busy caring for patients to provide frequent feedback during the project. In addition, the organization has a central PMO. As the project manager, you are required to provide specific project documentation (e.g., project charter, a detailed work breakdown and schedule, requirements and design documents, etc.) and gain approval via Stage Gates reviews for each phase to continue to the next phase. Finally, it's important that the system be fully functional and there is minimal downtime because if it is not near perfect at go-live, it could impact the quality of patient care.

Questions

1. What are some significant project variables that might impact your choice of a project management methodology?
2. Is there a case for using a hybrid methodology and if so, how would you implement it?

Feedback

Feedback for this case study can be found in the Appendix A.

Case Study 2: Implementation of an Organizational Metrics Dashboard

Type: Custom development

Additional Information

A small team made up of members from the matrixed organization has been assigned to build this new custom metrics dashboard. Executives are not exactly sure what they want, but they'll know it when they see it. There is pressure to "do something" and to produce innovative results quickly. The new CEO has asked for organizational performance metrics and is expecting modern analytics. Executive assistants (who will actually use the system to generate reports) have agreed to spend 25% of their time acting as product owners. You got certified as a Scrum Master recently and several of the developers have been involved in Scrum projects before, so you feel confident that the development team could handle an Agile project. The methodology has been used a few times, but it is still relatively new to the organization.

Questions

1. What are some significant project variables that might impact your choice of a project management methodology?
2. How will you handle stakeholders that don't understand the Agile development processes?

Feedback

Feedback for this case study can be found in Appendix A.

Chapter 8

Stakeholder Management

Grace Galvez Gonzalez

> It is the long history of humankind (and animal kind, too) that those who learned to collaborate and improvise most effectively have prevailed.

Charles Darwin

The success of a project lies in many areas of evaluation. Time and cost are factors that are often thought of first, but it is important to remember that they are not the only markers of satisfaction. The success of a project is influenced by its effect on people. The success of a project is also dependent on whether it creates a positive impact on the people it involves, the stakeholders.

Understanding who stakeholders are, how they think, and the best way to communicate with them is the heart of good stakeholder management. A project manager (PM) should consider what the project means to the stakeholder, how the project affects their responsibilities, and what the PM can do to make this implementation of the project a positive experience.

Stakeholder Identification

This process begins with stakeholder identification. A stakeholder is defined as any person who is affected by a project. A project manager must consider that:

- Stakeholders come from all levels of hierarchy. Stakeholders can be an executive overseeing the financial impact of a project, to the end user whose day-to-day tasks will be directly affected and everyone in between.

DOI: 10.4324/9781003206668-8

- Stakeholders are internal and external to the organization. Consider an IT project with an outside vendor implementing the new technology. Although the vendor isn't an internal member of the organization, they are connected to the project and impacted by its implementation.
- Stakeholders contribute to the success of a project. A satisfied stakeholder is an indication that the project is on track to meet their business need. Which leads to our last point.
- Stakeholder needs must be addressed and managed. To satisfy the stakeholder needs, a project manager must be aware of what is important to them.

Understanding these important resources starts with stakeholder identification. This is an ongoing process of taking inventory of everyone who will be impacted by the project. The identification begins during project initiation, continues throughout the project, and is the entire team's responsibility. A project manager will carefully sort and track their findings about stakeholders as they identify who they are. This will prove to be valuable information that should be kept readily available throughout the course of the project. These findings should include items such as their role within the project, their role within the organization, and their contact information. Every piece of information helps to paint a clearer picture.

Some types, or groups, of stakeholders are as follows:

- Executive leadership—the focus of this group is often related to how the project will meet the organization's strategic mission and goals within the available budget. They may also assist in the allocation of resources.
- Project sponsor(s)—the project may have one or more sponsors. For example, an IT project might have a technical sponsor, such as the chief information officer, and a business sponsor, such as the head of the department who will use the new system. Sponsors often have a high level of decision-making authority within the scope of the project. Their level of authority includes approval of the scope, any requested changes, and acceptance of the final deliverable at the end of the project. They may also be brought in to assist with the resolution of issues requiring escalation.

- End-users—members of this group will vary between projects. The focus of this group is the usability of the system, such as specific features, ease of use, and even system performance.
- External resources—members of this group include any outside organizations that are involved in the project. This can include the organization supplying a new commercial off-the-shelf (COTS) application, the vendor contracted to develop a custom application, or the consulting company providing supplemental staffing. The provider of a legacy system that is being replaced is also a stakeholder, since you may not have a relationship with them once their system is no longer in use.
- Project manager—this is a very challenging and high-profile role that is often completely accountable for the success of the project. Because project managers facilitate stakeholder analysis, they often do not think of themselves in this role.
- Project team—each member of the project team has a stake in the project and will influence its success. They may be fully dedicated to working on the project or they might need to balance work on the project against their regular job duties. The latter is seen more often wherein the team members must balance supporting other systems while implementing a new one or possibly working on multiple projects at the same time.
- Functional/department managers—these stakeholders are often focused on how the project will impact their department and their staff. The end users may report to them, or they might be end users themselves. Their department might be impacted though workflow changes, data flow changes, or having their staff pulled from normal work to help with the project as a workgroup member or fully assigned as a member of the project team.
- Committees—there may be a number of committees that have an interest, or stake, in the success of the project. These may include the governance committee, steering committees, or even a board of directors for the organization.

Some stakeholders can be managed as a group with similar goals such as the end-users, while others will be specifically identified with a defined role. These are your key stakeholders. These critical resources are named individuals who will require focused attention and whose satisfaction is essential to the success of a project.

There are many ways to identify the stakeholders for a project. Any past project that is similar in scope or had the same impact can be used by reviewing the project's historical information. This would include the stakeholder analysis, communication plan, charter, or scope. The sponsor or members of the project team are also good resources as it is everyone's responsibility to help with the identification.

The exercise of identifying these resources serves not only as an inventory process, but as a reminder that identifying and managing stakeholders is not an exact science. The names and roles may be different depending on the organization, the status of the project, and any changes that come though the life cycle of a project. The project manager must stay flexible and ready to shift their approach toward any of the stakeholders of a project. Once the initial group has been identified, typically during initiation or planning, the project manager can move them through the process of stakeholder analysis. This process will unlock the best way to successfully communicate with each individual or group.

Stakeholder Analysis

Stakeholder analysis is the process in which the project manager evaluates each stakeholder, or stakeholder group, to understand their perception of the project and how they can help or hinder the process and work being done. This analysis also provides key details about what information and communication methods are most valuable to them. This process allows the project manager to see the project from the perspective of each stakeholder including those who do not have a positive perception of the project. In doing this, they will be able to determine the most successful way to communicate with each stakeholder and accommodate their needs. While the analysis is often completed during the planning process group, it should be reviewed and updated as new stakeholders are identified or additional information becomes known.

The project manager should understand the following about the stakeholders.

■ Their interest in the project
■ Their expectation of the project and the project manager
■ Their desired relationship with the project and project team, or how involved do they want to be

- Their commitment to the project and project team members
- Their communication style for both sending and receiving information
- Their desired outcome from the project

TIP

Stakeholder identification and analysis should be done early and reviewed often.

Stakeholder analysis involves four areas of evaluation. While this information may be easier to understand for individuals, it is often more difficult when assessing groups.

1. Focus of energy: what part of the project is this stakeholder invested in? End-users probably won't be focused on the cost of the project, but they are probably highly invested in the implementation process or final deliverable.
2. Information intake: how do they view the information they receive? Is the stakeholder focused on the big picture, or do they prefer to dive deep into the details of the project? Is this person focused on facts and the current moment of the project or are they more interested in looking toward the future and what other possibilities lie ahead? The PM should understand what information they want, how they want to receive it, and the frequency.
3. Process: how can they provide what the project needs to be successful? How can the project manager provide them what they need to be successful? Consider not only their way of thinking, but the practical channels of communication as well, such as emails versus meetings or calls.
4. Life approach: this is closely tied to the information intake process, but it is far more subtle. This portion of the analysis is best gathered via observation. Here the project manager will consider how this person views the world and modify their approach to be the most effective. For example, if the person tends to look for the flaws in the world, the communication should aim to focus on the details that show the soundness of the project. The project manager must

be thoughtful in the gathering of this type of data and consider the culture of the organization. It's important to be respectful and aware of power dynamics within the organization and what is proper to speak out loud, or what is best observed and taken note of in a more subtle approach.

A project manager can use personality assessments to gather data about those involved in the project. These tools can reveal insights into the project team. The PM can also use their existing knowledge to find traits through interactions. Are they an introvert, are they objective in their decision-making process, do they like to take in information and brainstorm about solutions, or do they want all options presented before making any decisions? Having formal results may not be needed to understand key traits. Observation of behavior can be just as effective.

As we gather information about who the stakeholders are through identification, and learn about them through stakeholder analysis, it is a good idea to record these findings for ongoing reference throughout the project and as historical information for future projects. This helps to outline how best to manage them as individuals or groups. A tool such as the one in Table 8.1 provides a way to document the outputs of the analysis in a way that provides quick access to the details. Some organizations expect this information to be in a more formal document, in those cases, the table would provide a summary of the contents.

Another tool that is beneficial for reference is in Figure 8.1, where the stakeholders are defined by different dimensions. These are typically based on their levels of power, support, influence, and need, related to the project. This tool allows for the analysis of two dimensions at a time, such as power and interest. It allows the project manager to further enrich the findings of the analysis through the use of a visual aid which can be updated as new information becomes known.

The stakeholder matrix is an at-a-glance representation, or output, of stakeholder analysis. Each stakeholder is added to the matrix based on the information gathered in the analysis. This is used to help the project manager determine the best way to manage them.

Table 8.1 Sample Stakeholder Analysis Template

Stakeholder	Involvement / Interest in Project	Level of Influence	Level of Impact	Decision-making Authority	Expectations	Plan for Managing Expectations	Level of Support	Plan for Enhancing Support

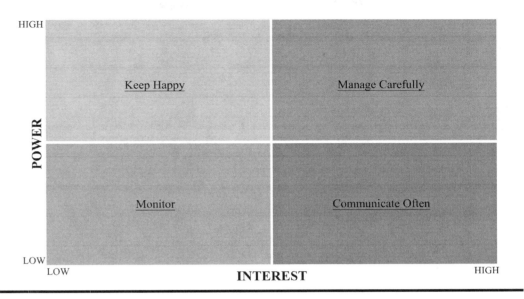

Figure 8.1   Stakeholder matrix.

Let's consider an end-user. The project is to implement a process to change how the radiology department annotates studies. The new process has been approved by the sponsor(s). One radiologist, Michelle, has been very involved in the development of the new process and in leading the way to communicate it to the rest of the department. Due to her unofficial leadership role in the department, her power level would be high on the matrix. Her level of interest is very high and would affect where she lands on the matrix. We want to be sure not to neglect sharing information with this stakeholder, and we want to consider that although they don't have explicit power, they can help create a smoother path to the implementation process. We also want to be mindful not to over-invest in this stakeholder more than we would in someone who falls into the Manage Carefully section of the matrix. In Figure 8.2, you can see where Michelle, among others, lands in the completed stakeholder matrix.

The stakeholder matrix highlights how the project manager and team should invest resources for managing and communicating. During the project, stakeholders can move from one quadrant to another based on new information or potentially a scope change that adjusts their views about the project.

It's important to remember that a stakeholder analysis has other benefits beyond the immediate communication types toward stakeholders. The outcome of the analysis also helps us understand and manage

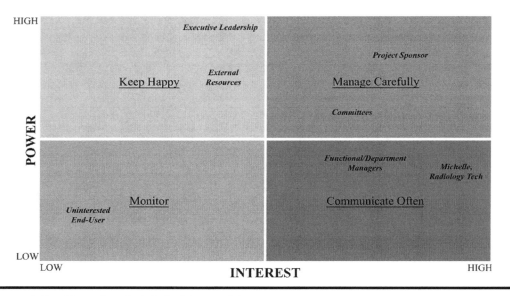

Figure 8.2 Completed stakeholder matrix.

their expectations. By understanding the area of focus, interest, and life approach, the project manager will see what is important to the stakeholder and discover the most effective way to manage their expectations. The stakeholder analysis, and tools, are also beneficial as historical information, as mentioned above. When the opportunity arises to work with a stakeholder again on a different project, the analysis and all outputs can help the project manager see where they stood in the past and provide good information to help with the identification and analysis process for the new project. This historical information also allows the project manager to see if this stakeholder is consistent with their approach or if their interest and power have shifted.

Through interactions with others, the project manager can gather details about their perceptions of others and the project. Do they have the view that "they" are against "us," this could be the difference between the business and information technology (IT) or the organization and outside stakeholders such as vendors, providers, or even government with defined regulations? It is important to help bridge this divide when present. An integrated project team and ensuring all viewpoints are heard can help to improve these perceptions. Another approach is to ensure the communications include terminology that is understood by the intended audience. While the messages may have the same content, the way they are worded needs to be specific to those receiving the message.

TIP

Present to the intended audience, using their terminology, so they will understand the message.

Now that the project manager has taken stock of who the stakeholders are, how to best communicate with them, and how much energy is needed to manage them, the project manager can develop a communication plan.

Communication Plan

A communication plan is a comprehensive document that defines who, what, when, where, and how communication will happen for the entire project. Information gathered during stakeholder identification and analysis will make building out the communication plan much easier. This plan will create a touchstone for the project manager to ensure all stakeholders receive the information they need, when they need it and in the proper format.

The communication plan can be as robust as a lengthy document describing all communication to be done during the project and how each will be accomplished. It can be as simple as a table with columns for the details, see Table 8.2. The project manager, with input from the rest of the team and sponsor(s), identifies what communication is needed as a starting point. This communication may be related to the status of project tasks, information about training, the new workflows, the schedule, or details about the go-live. Stakeholders can get involved in the project through meetings to discuss requirements, current or future workflows, process redesign as well as participation in user acceptance testing. All of these involved sharing of information and should be included in the communication plan.

The information gathered during the stakeholder analysis will provide key information to completing the communication plan. The project manager will identify what information each stakeholder needs, wants, and their expectations on how and when to receive it. It is important to note that while the project manager is the main focal point for communication, there

Table 8.2 Sample Communication Plan

Who	What	When	How	Responsible
Board/Steering Committee	1. Project status 2. Issues requiring escalation	1. Monthly 2. As needed	1. Verbal at Meetings 2. Verbal at Meetings or email	PM
Project Sponsors	1. Project status 2. Issues requiring escalation	1. Weekly 2. Issues reported daily	1. Status report sent via email 2. Include in status report and via email as needed	PM
End Users	1. Project status 2. Info regarding system changes 3. Training information 4. Go-live details	1. Monthly 2. Monthly, June-August 3. Monthly, weekly in July-August 4. Monthly July-August	1. Chief Information Officer (CIO) Newsletter email 2. Town Hall meetings 3. CIO Newsletter email and flyers 4. CIO Newsletter email and emails	1. CIO, info from PM 2. CIO and PM 3. CIO, info from PM 4. CIO, info from PM
Help Desk	1. Application information required to support post-live	1. August, 2 weeks prior to go-live	1. Group meeting	PM and Help Desk Mgr
Project Team	1. Project status 2. Issue status and resolutions 3. Activities details	1. Weekly 2. Weekly, more frequently as needed 3. Weekly	1. Status meetings 2. Verbal in person or email 3. Status meetings	PM
Project Manager	1. Status on activities 2. Issues, new and status on current	1. As they change 2. As identified and as changed	1. Status meetings, 2. Verbal in person, Email	Team Members
Project Manager	1. Decisions impacting project 2. Issue status/resolution if escalated	1. As decided 2. As status changes	1. Email, verbal in person 2. Email, verbal in person	Project Sponsors

is a need for most stakeholders to communicate to the project manager at various points in the project.

The basic elements that a communication plan should include are:

■ Who are your stakeholders? Be clear about the stakeholder's role within the project, not their title or role in the organization.

■ What information does the stakeholder need and what do they want? While it's important to create a culture of transparency to instill trust, you want to be sure not to bombard a stakeholder with information that isn't relevant to their role.

■ How often does the stakeholder need or expect updated information? The stakeholder matrix will be the key to getting this right. Just as it is important to share the right of information, it is also key not bombard them with information often that they stop paying attention. You also don't want to leave a stakeholder who wants constant updates without the information they need to feel confident in the project.

■ What is your vehicle for sharing information with the stakeholder? Channels of communication are vast and varied. While some stakeholders may prefer an email summary, others may need a verbal update that can be passed along quickly. Town hall meetings where general project information can be shared will help to reach larger audiences to keep them informed.

■ Who is responsible for the communication? It is easy for the project manager to assign the task of communication to themselves, but it is important to remember that often, another member of the project may be the best person to speak to a group of stakeholders. Delegate this task accordingly and make sure they have the details they need to complete the task.

The communication plan should be comprehensive without becoming a burden to support. The best approach is to remember the basic tenets of contribution, interest, and focus.

The amount a stakeholder contributes to the project will affect the communication they need. Sometimes, they are affected by the project outcome but are not a contributor. This group of stakeholders will need to receive information about the status and be made to feel included. It is important to provide guidance and awareness to this group that a change is coming without overwhelming them with information that will get in the way of their other job duties.

Interest in a project will also impact communication. Is the stakeholder invested in the minute details of the project or are they looking for a high-level overview of what's being done? It may be very important to supply exact details of technical developments to a stakeholder who is a member of the IT department, but an executive member may not want more than hearing that the development exists and that it's progressing on schedule.

It's important to remember that tools like the matrix will provide a view of how invested the stakeholder is in the project, but the project manager must also consider what areas of the project the stakeholder is interested in. The stakeholder may have a perspective that is focused internally to the organization or their department where their interest is in what this project will do within the organization. Or a stakeholder may be completely externally focused and want to know how this project will affect those outside of the organizations, such as patients or insurance providers.

High interest and high contribution coupled with a stakeholder who needed careful management may require consistent and detailed information. A stakeholder who just needs enough to keep them happy may not want more than a summary of the project periodically. However, it is important to keep in mind that you want to deliver complete information. It is up to the project manager to provide accurate and consistent information to all.

Once types of information are established, the channels of communication should also be considered. These can be conventional as a scope document, meeting minutes, and any other shared documentation or they can be non-traditional such as flyers, bulletin board announcements, or even overhead announcements. Other things to consider are town halls or dress rehearsals for launch or taking part in the existing department or shift meetings.

It's important to remember that all communication, regardless of channels, should deliver a consistent message. Consider the color scheme of documents, font choices, or a logo mark to help instantly figure out what communication is regarding. Although the methods may change, creating a clear identity for the project is key to recognition and building a sense of familiarity with the project.

The purpose of communication and the communication plan is to create availability, transparency, and consistency. When looking to share information, the PM and the project team should consider the best way to reach everyone involved and affected by the project. This builds confidence in the project and encourages the team to invest in the success of the project.

TIP

It is up to the project manager to phrase information accurately, consistently, at the correct level of detail, and using terminology that is understood.

Stakeholder Management in Action

A project manager can use the insights gained about stakeholders to help develop measures of success for the project. With the information learned through the stakeholder analysis and communication planning, the project manager can help guide the how the project will be measured based on if the business need was met. Understanding what matters to the stakeholder and their definition of success will be crucial throughout the process of evaluating if the project was successful. Measures of success is further discussed in Chapter 11.

The project manager can also take this opportunity to address the goals of each stakeholder and connect in a way that is familiar to the stakeholder. The understanding of each stakeholder's cultural approach can also help the project manager in serving the role of diplomat amongst the stakeholders. Project managers aim to address the concerns and needs of each stakeholder and bridge any gaps between stakeholders so that everyone is striving toward the same finish line without feeling that their needs have been neglected. It is important to note that not all goals and expectations may be able to be met within the scope of the project. The sponsor(s) can help with managing unrealistic expectations.

Stakeholder management is an active process throughout the life of the project. The level of a stakeholder's involvement or views may change through the project. While it is important to still properly manage that stakeholder, it is necessary to consider what type of management they now require. Conversely, a new project stakeholder may arise in the middle of a project. It's possible to realize that a stakeholder from a specific skillset is missing and needs to be introduced to the project. If so, it is important to run this new stakeholder through the process of analysis and placement on the stakeholder matrix to see where they belong on the communication plan.

Remember that stakeholder management revolves around the idea of how to properly involve and deliver information based on a stakeholder's needs and the project's needs. Here we use the concept of telling a story. The goal is to deliver a comprehensive and succinct distillation of information that is relevant to the stakeholder based on the information learned through the identification and analyzation process. Cultivate a truthful message that is short, sweet, consistent, to the point and complete. Be sure your message aligns with the stakeholder expectations.

Case Study 1: Implementation of an Electronic Health Record

Type: Commercial off-the-shelf

Additional Information

The project includes the emergency department (ED) and will include new workflows for clinical documentation by the nurses.

Questions

1. Who are the stakeholders?
2. What types of communication should be included in the project?
3. What is the best method of communication for each?

Feedback

Feedback for this case study can be found in Appendix A.

Case Study 2: Implementation of a Research Tracking System

Type: Custom development

Additional Information

The new research tracking system includes users from four different protocols. It has been requested to keep the workflows the same for all protocols, current and future. This will improve the ability to extend the use in the future without needing to customize for each group.

Questions

1. Who are the stakeholders?
2. What types of communication should be included in the project?
3. What is the best method of communication for each?

Feedback

Feedback for this case study can be found in Appendix A.

Chapter 9

System Configuration

> Lack of direction, not lack of time, is the problem. We all have twenty-four-hour days.
>
> **Zig Ziglar**

Some say project managers do not necessarily need to have any knowledge of the industry, or subject, of the project to manage it. Others respond that while it is not necessary, it is beneficial to have at least a basic understanding to have credibility with project team members and to know what to ask and how to gauge the answers.

To fulfill this latter skill set, this chapter will provide an overview of the more common technical concepts and terms used when implementing software. In addition to the information provided here, it is highly beneficial to also find one or two people who can serve as references, providing explanations of unknown concepts and terms as the project progresses. This source of information does not necessarily need to be a member of the project team.

TIP

Project managers should be able to trust their project team members to be the Subject Matter Experts (SMEs). Unfortunately, project managers rarely get to choose their team members.

DOI: 10.4324/9781003206668-9

Workstations

When implementing a new system, the project team should evaluate the availability of workstations for the users. This should include the locations at which the systems will be used. If there are workstations present in this location, are they correctly situated and configured to fit with the workflow? If additional workstations are needed, is there space, is there power, and is network access available? Further, do the current workstations meet the specifications of the system? For example, a picture archiving and communication system (PACS) used to view electronic radiology images may require extra memory and a high-resolution monitor. An alternative to the traditional workstation comes with the expanded use of mobile devices in healthcare which is discussed below.

Mobile devices are becoming more prevalent in healthcare and provide a unique challenge to the information technology department. These devices can be smart phones or tablets. They are mobile and are carried around as the users complete their work and may even go home with them. The biggest benefit is access to information where it is needed or wherever the user is at the time. The challenges are multiple. Will the data be readable on a smaller screen? Can the necessary security and privacy controls be applied to the device? How will you prevent theft of the device? How will you protect the data if they are lost or stolen? Most of the system vendors are beginning to offer mobile applications that connect to their system where the data are displayed appropriately for a mobile device. There are many mobile device management systems available today that will help with the security, privacy, and loss management questions. These systems provide the ability to monitor, track, and remotely wipe mobile devices, as needed.

Client

A client is an application that enables a user (human, service, interface) to access the central information store or database. This access can be requested by a human using the system, a service requesting data, or an interface requesting or sending data. This is essentially the client-server model, which will be further defined later in this chapter. The client makes requests, whether to send or receive data, and the server satisfies that request.

A thin client is a computer or application that relies on other hardware for most of the traditional computational work. The end user accesses the system through a low-end computer terminal, or dumb terminal, while the server provides the processing and storage functionality. These devices can be used in a client-server model where the client application is located on the server rather than the workstation.

Multiple thin clients can access the same server to run the application. The benefits of this technology are lower cost and easier maintenance of the terminal workstations. Updates to the system only need to be made on the server rather than to each individual workstations. While the server is very robust and can handle multiple clients, the performance tends to be variable, depending on the application, configuration, and infrastructure. The server can become a single point of failure.

The thinnest clients are remote desktop applications where the systems are running on a centrally hosted virtual workstation. A basic example of a thin client is an Internet browser connected to a website. A thin client can be platform independent, which means the user is not restricted to only using a specific type of computer or operating system. There are a variety of vendors who can provide thin client technology for the healthcare industry. If the user is on the organization's network, they may not need any special hardware or software to access the system and to receive or send data.

The contrast is the traditional thick or fat client, in which most processing and storage functions for the system are done by the workstation, rather than by relying on other hardware. These systems usually require higher processing power and high-resolution graphics cards. This option is a better choice for multimedia performance and offers improved client performance, in most cases. However, client updates will need to be applied to each workstation, increasing the workload for maintenance and increasing the risk of software or hardware conflicts on each client. Depending on the specific application, it is possible to utilize a workstation management tool to push the updates to all devices. Either way, this can add substantial overhead to application support costs and work effort, depending on the number of workstations requiring updates.

Servers

A server is a high-end computer, or series of computers, that provides essential services across a network. Often, they have a dedicated functionality, such as a print server, file server, web server, or a database server. They require a steady power supply and network connection.

They tend to be noisy and generate heat while needing to remain within a specified temperature range, which is why they are often housed in a dedicated room called a datacenter or server room. These rooms are equipped with redundant power supply and control systems to monitor and moderate temperatures, humidity, and other environmental factors.

When multiple servers are logically connected through a dedicated high-speed network connection, this is referred to as a cluster, and each server is referred to as a node on the cluster. This is used to provide server redundancy or load balancing wherein traffic is balanced between the two or more clustered servers, decreasing the workload of each. In a hospital, or hospital system, a server cluster may include many servers (nodes), which allows a portion of the cluster to be brought down without impacting the user's access. This is useful when applying software updates or other maintenance.

In addition to easing software maintenance, distributing the workload across multiple servers expedites the computing processes and prioritizes tasks and scheduling or rescheduling them based on priority and user demand. Clustering also provides high availability for the system. Each server within the cluster has the ability to take over for the other, if necessary due to failure of a node. Clustering servers can provide many benefits but be aware that not all applications are cluster aware or have the ability to utilize a clustered environment.

Storage Area Network

A storage area network (SAN) is a remote data storage device connected to servers that appears to be locally attached. A SAN typically has its own network connection that runs only between itself and the main servers. System availability is further enhanced if the SAN has redundant storage to mitigate the risk of a SAN storage bank failure. The Fiber Channel fabric is a specially designed infrastructure to handle SAN communication. The access is much faster and more reliable than normal network protocols. This storage management solution provides increased flexibility, speed, and scalability, but tends to be expensive.

Disaster Recovery

As is true of anyone leading an enterprise, project managers need to understand disaster recovery. This refers to how to recover your business from a disaster when the application, data, or the entire system is made unavailable.

While full destruction of the data center can be considered a disaster, most often, recovery is necessary when there are more localized problems, such as broken water pipes causing water damage, hardware failures, database corruption, or a small fire. Disaster recovery includes everything from performing regularly scheduled backups to having disaster recovery standby sites. Each system should have a disaster recovery plan that outlines the activities to be taken in order to minimize the duration of loss of access and the steps to recover the system and its data. This plan should also include the acceptable recovery time and how this will be met if disaster occurs. The plan should be rehearsed at least once or twice a year to ensure it is realistic and achievable.

A backup is a duplicate, archive, or copy of some or all of the data in a system to a separate location on the network or to some form of media, such as magnetic tape or CD. A full backup is the backup of all data and is often completed nightly, when usage is lower. An incremental backup is a procedure that backs up only data that has changed since the last backup. These can be scheduled at various times during the day and are less of a load on the performance of the system.

After a catastrophic failure of the system, data can be recovered by restoring the last full backup plus each incremental backup that followed in the order they were created. Any changes made to the system after the last incremental backup will be lost. The frequency of the incremental backups must be weighed against the impact on end-user performance.

Disaster recovery sites are remote locations where impacted systems can be recovered. These are used to mitigate the risk of the current location becoming unusable. There are a variety of options depending on the acceptable recovery time. More critical systems may need to be recovered within 4 to 8 hours, while other systems may be able to wait 24 hours or more. A cold site is simply a location dedicated to this purpose. All hardware necessary for recovery must be procured, delivered, and set up before the recovery process can begin. Without this being done ahead, the delay in recovery to a cold site can be substantial.

A better idea is a warm site that is set up with the necessary hardware that is close to matching what is in the current datacenter. The backups must be delivered, or made accessible, prior to restoring any system. Best of all is a hot site, which has all necessary hardware plus a near-complete image of the current data with the systems waiting for the last backup of data to be restored. Hot sites are very expensive but provide the quickest recovery time. In any case, a cost–benefit analysis should be completed prior to choosing the type of recovery site. Also, it is important to understand that not all systems within the datacenter need to have the same disaster recovery strategy.

Along with a disaster recovery plan, an organization should have a business continuity plan. This defines how the business will continue when the system is unavailable and includes any downtime procedures, paper forms, and recovery processes. For example, how will laboratory orders be handled without a system to place the order, print the labels, communicate the order to the laboratory, and communicate the results back to the patient care area? The recovery processes should include what data will be entered into the system when it is back available and who is responsible for entering this data. Will paper forms be scanned, or will the information be manually entered? The business continuity plan is an important part of disaster recovery planning and should be followed for any project activation which requires the system to be unavailable, such as an upgrade to the electronic health record (EHR).

High Availability

High availability is a system design intended to achieve the highest level of availability possible for a system. More complex systems have more potential points of failure, which result in a higher risk. Redundancy provides a reliable alternative if something fails; an example is a backup power supply for power outages. The concept of redundancy can be applied to most components of any system, from the network to file storage.

As mentioned earlier in this chapter, clustered servers provide redundancy—if one node fails, the work processes failover to the others in the cluster without impacting the users. However, as with disaster recovery, redundancy can be expensive and should be considered based on a cost–benefit analysis for the most critical systems.

Network

A network is a connection between multiple computers and other hardware, such as servers and printers, allowing them to communicate with each other and share resources. There are many options for network hardware, from fiber optics, cellular, ethernet, to wireless. The majority of hardware will be connected to the network through direct connection with an ethernet cable.

This is used for any computer or printer that will remain in a single location and provides a consistent, reliable, connection. Ethernet is frequently deployed using other devices such as hubs, switches, or routers to join multiple smaller networks together. These devices reside in network closets located throughout a building.

External facing websites or web-based applications should be located in a demilitarization zone (DMZ). This is a separate location of the network that sits between the public internet and the organization's private network. It provides protection for the organization's internal systems from untrusted traffic by limiting access from outside the network.

With the introduction of electronic documentation comes the need to have computers that are available where patients are located. With most facilities, there is not room or the budget to put a computer at each bedside. Wireless workstations that reside on a cart are one solution; they can be taken wherever they are needed. They were initially called computers on wheels (COWs) and are now called workstations on wheels (WOWs) because some found the term COW could be offensive if taken out of context. While WOWs can be taken anywhere, they can access the network only where a signal is available. A wireless network survey evaluates the current wireless network and provides a mapping of where there are gaps with no signal. This outlines where additional access points should be placed to provide the best coverage with the least quantity of dead zones, where no signal is available. The wireless network is also important for the increased demand for mobile workstations.

With the expanding use of mobile devices and laptops by patients and visitors, many organizations are providing them with a separate wireless network. To ensure the security of the networks used for the organization's systems, mobile devices, and even laboratory instruments, a guest network is set up. This allows patients and visitors access to the Internet while keeping them away from the network used for the business.

Interface

The term interface refers to the interaction between two components. This can be the interaction between an input device, such as a keyboard, with a processing device, such as a computer. An interface could also refer to the interaction between the user and a system, such as the screen design or graphical user interface (GUI).

This section will define an interface as a connection between two systems. For example, when a physician enters an order in the EHR for a specific laboratory test, the system would process the order and send a message to an interface engine, which then sends the message to the laboratory system. Once the specimen has been collected and processed by the laboratory, a second interface message would send the results of the test back to the EHR for the patient care team to review.

These messages are often processed through an interoperability standard called Health Level 7 (HL7) developed by the Health Level Seven International organization, founded in 1987. HL7 provides a standard framework for the structure of the interface messages where the data are stored in specific, consistent, segments of the message.

Interfaces can be developed to process and send messages that are triggered by an event. In the example just given, placement of the order is the trigger. This is called a real-time interface, since the information is sent in real time when the trigger occurs. The message would include a defined set of data. In the example of the laboratory order, the HL7 message might include data such as the patient's name, medical record number, date of birth, laboratory test(s) ordered, and any special instructions. If translation is needed, such as when the source system has patient first name and last name, but the destination system is expecting patient full name, an interface engine is used to modify the data in the message between the two.

Another option for an interface is to schedule a message(s) for every so many hours or once daily. This is accomplished by developing a query to look for something specific, and if the criteria is met, a message is sent to the destination system. An example of this type of interface could be a query right before each meal to determine any changes in the patient's location since the last query. If there was a change, a message would be sent to the nutrition system with the updated location, so meals are delivered to the patient's current location at mealtime. This type of an interface is sometimes referred to as a data feed, since it is feeding data at specific times of the day and is not based on a trigger.

Interfaces are also used to populate data from devices such as monitors, ventilators, or laboratory instruments. While this type of integration is often dependent on the vendor or the age of the devices, the steps for analysis and development follow a similar process as between two systems. Mapping documents should be used to define requirements and an interface engine is typically required.

When an interface is involved in a software implementation, it is very important to make sure the requirements are properly documented. This would include what data are to be sent and in what location or segment of the message. The format of the data being sent must also be defined. A mapping document is used to show how the data will appear in the message leaving the source system, if any manipulation will be done in an interface engine, and finally how the data will appear when the destination system receives the message. The technical staff supporting each system must approve these requirements to ensure they can work with the data as defined.

Environments

When implementing software, it is rarely as easy as putting a CD in the drive, or downloading it, and loading the application on your personal home computer. They are complicated and require time to design, develop, and implement. Testing will need to occur, preferably before any training that is scheduled.

Often, development, testing, and training activities occur simultaneously, especially during normal operations and maintenance. How will each of these activities impact each other if they occur in the same environment or instance of the system? Some say, "There is no test like production," but would you really want to use your live production system to do testing or training—probably not. In this section, the different environments will be reviewed. It is not necessary to have each of these for every software implementation, but a decision needs to be made early in the project planning phase regarding which ones will be utilized.

Sandbox

A sandbox environment is used for play. This is often used to experiment with changes when the impact is unclear or if it is unknown if the system has the functionality for the change. This is a stand-alone system that has limited extras such as printing or any interfaces. Only test data should be entered to verify the impact of any changes, and this environment should be refreshed periodically to clear out unwanted changes and test data. A sandbox is also used when developing software to provide a workspace to develop code in isolation, often after which the changes are merged with other code.

Development

As the name states, this environment is used for development. The work completed in this environment should be approved through documented requirements and/or change requests. Once the changes are made, they are validated to ensure they were done correctly through unit testing. For example, if the list of allergy types is added to a drop-down menu through the use of a configuration tool, the developer should validate that the end user will see the list in the appropriate field and that the entries are in the expected order, either alphabetically or with the most common at the top.

This is often a stand-alone system similar to sandbox and should only have test data entered. It is a good practice to refresh this environment with a copy of production once or twice a year to keep their configurations in synch. When this is done, the real patient data should be removed prior to use to ensure proper privacy controls.

Test

Once changes are verified in the development environment, they are moved to the test environment. This is where all the testing occurs and should be set up similar to production with test versions of any interfaces. These test interfaces should connect to the test environments of the other systems. This will allow full integration testing of the messages crossing between the two systems. Test printers should be set up to verify any report or printing functionality.

There are many ways to migrate the changes from the development to the test environment. The test can be refreshed with a copy of development at regular intervals; the changes can be unloaded from development and then loaded into the test, or they can be manually migrated. Often, the method chosen is directly related to the type of change and the options available within the system.

For some smaller systems, the decision might be made to have a combined development and test environment. This provides the advantage of keeping only one environment in synch with production. The disadvantage is that testing is occurring while other changes are being made in the same system, which might invalidate the test results. The work effort for keeping extra environments in synch and migrating the changes should be weighed against the volume of changes and testing when deciding if separate environments are necessary or desired.

Preproduction

Some testing requires an environment identical to production. Preproduction is a copy of production with all real data retained and having full functionality, such as interfaces and printing. This is where testing can really be "like production." While production offers the best way to test exactly what end users will experience, there is an element of risk when testing in production. However, preproduction provides this opportunity without risk. Having a full-size database also allows for performance and load testing. This environment does require a full copy of production, including hardware and interfaces. Additional security controls should be added to this environment since it does include production data.

Production

The production environment is where the end users actually do their work and use the system as it is intended. Real data are entered continuously through direct data entry or via interfaces bringing information in from other systems. This is the most important environment and must remain available and reliable for the users. As tested changes are migrated into this environment, the testing step is to validate that they were migrated correctly. Full testing has already been completed so validation of the migration is all that should be needed.

Training

There are a variety of ways to train end users in how to use the new system. If the training plan calls for any hands-on experience, a training environment should be considered. This is a static version of the system with defined training data that match the training materials. Generic training accounts are configured to provide specific access for the different classes. If the students will be entering data, the database should be refreshed regularly to clear out the extra information entered during the class. This allows each class to start at the same point. Training and training planning are further discussed in Chapter 12.

Considerations

When making a decision on which environments are right for the specific software being implemented, the project team needs to weigh the risks against the budget and available resources to support each throughout operations and maintenance. For smaller systems in which there will be minimal changes, a combined development and test environment along with production may be all that is needed. If the department using this small system has a very low turnover of staff, they might not need a training environment. When it is expected that there will be a need for ongoing training for new employees, such as for an EHR, a training environment might be necessary and desired.

Each environment needs to be maintained with updates, requested changes, and vendor fixes related to the system, database, and even the operating system, third-party software, and antivirus on the servers or workstations. This takes time and resources to complete and must be repeated for each environment.

There is also the cost and maintenance of the hardware, network, and storage for the databases. Some environments can be hosted on the same hardware, such as the development and test environments on the same server or cluster. This can save some cost for hardware, but updates that are related to the hardware or systems on the servers will be applied to all environments at the same time. This is one reason why production should always be on its own hardware. This physical separation allows testing of all changes prior to production implementation.

The evaluation of options and final decision of how the system will be configured should occur during the project planning phase so the associated activities are scheduled, and each environment is ready and available when needed.

Case Study 1: Implementation of an Electronic Health Record

Type: Commercial off-the-shelf

Additional Information

Your analysis of the current situation shows that there are a few workstations in the nurse's stations with a single printer. No other workstations or printers are available except in offices.

The project scope includes protocol order sets that will be sending orders to pharmacy, laboratory, and radiology systems. It also includes alerts related to the opioid management monitoring program.

Questions

1. What environments would you anticipate you might need?
2. Would you anticipate the need for redundancy and disaster recovery for this system?
3. What might be some considerations when evaluating workstations and printers for the end users?

Feedback

Feedback for this case study can be found in Appendix A.

Case Study 2: Implementation of a Research Tracking System

Type: Custom development

Additional Information

Your analysis of the current situation shows that each of the users has access to a computer and printer. Most utilize a personal computer, while a few are using Mac workstations.

It is expected that each user will enter his or her own research data as they are gathered.

Senior leadership would like to see the most current data in the dashboard whenever they log in.

Questions

1. What environments would you anticipate you might need?
2. Would you anticipate the need for redundancy and disaster recovery for this system?
3. What might be some considerations when evaluating workstations and printers for the end users?

Feedback

Feedback for this case study can be found in Appendix A.

Chapter 10

Security and Privacy

Bob Eichler

> Treat your password like your toothbrush. Don't let anybody else
> use it, and get a new one every six months.
>
> **Clifford Stoll**

Security and privacy controls are important for healthcare information technology (IT) systems. When implementing or modifying an electronic medical record, or any system containing; Protected Health Information (PHI), Personally Identifiable Information (PII), or Payment Card Information (PCI), the project manager must include the information security office and privacy office in the project team. In recent years, healthcare IT systems have been targeted by hackers and criminal organizations. Similar to the banking and credit card industries, healthcare systems store massive amounts of personal data and can be money makers for cyber criminals, and as a result are subject to a number of regulatory obligations that dictate functions or procedures the systems must possess. Over the course of the last several years, numerous hospitals and physician practices (as well as other business, government entities, and private individuals) have been targeted by malicious software (Ransomware) which rendered their electronic medical record system, ancillary systems, and general office files unavailable for business operations until a ransom was paid or cybersecurity experts were hired to recover and restore their systems from backup copies or their disaster recovery sites. Failure to secure systems can have a serious, negative impact on an organization's reputation and financial health.

Criminals will target any company or system from which they believe they will be able to extract sensitive data. The sensitive data could be

DOI: 10.4324/9781003206668-10

PHI, PII, PCI, or other company-sensitive information such as intellectual property or strategic plans. Even organizational charts have value. From PHI/PCI/PII, criminals will extract (to sell or exploit) things such as patient names, medical identification numbers, and health insurance information. Aside of various identity theft scheme, criminals may submit payment requests to private medical insurers and the Health and Human Services (HHS) Centers for Medicaid and Medicare Services (CMS) for fraudulent tests and services. In many cases, the hospital or physician practice is unaware of a breach until patients report errors in their medical history or medical insurance. This criminal activity can go undetected for a year or more. Unfortunately, the investigation, recovery, and correction of the patient's medical history can take equally as long to restore.

The criminals may even take your org chart, and when combined with information extracted from social media, attempt to trick people inside your company to approve fraudulent wire transfers. The range of attempted exploits is only limited by the criminals' imagination.

To understand the extent of the security threats facing healthcare entities, one may view the reported breaches of protected health information (PHI) on the US Department of Health and Human Services Office for Civil Rights (OCR) Breach Portal. In 2015, there were 30 reported breaches affecting 500 or more individuals by healthcare providers related to hacking/IT Incidents. In 2020, there were 533 breaches affecting 500 or more individuals. The volume of breaches has increased 17 times, in just five years. Most breaches are preventable with appropriate security controls and monitoring. Once a breach occurs, it is expensive and lengthy process for the healthcare organizations to investigate and correct. If patient data are involved, the organization must notify the OCR and follow breach notification guidance to tell the patient about the breach as well as steps he or she can take to protect his or her identity and sensitive information. This public disclosure of a breach may result in patients and physicians thinking twice about the privacy of their personal information. If patients have options to seek care from other hospitals and physicians, they may take their business elsewhere, which can negatively impact the bottom line of the organization following a breach. If an audit by OCR reveals that standards of care for protecting PHI were not followed, it can impose monetary fines, civil, and criminal liability on the organization. Penalties where "wilful neglect" is determined by OCR, can go as high as $1,500,000.

TIP

Cybersecurity should be included in planning for all health IT systems.

It is easier and less expensive to implement security controls during the initial implementation of an IT system rather than try to add technical controls just prior to the activation. If it is even possible to implement these controls, you will certainly miss your original move to production dates. It may require the addition of encryption, changes in server configuration, network configuration, adding authentication and authorization controls, adjustments or additions to system or application logging details, and additional testing. Protecting the privacy of PHI requires good security and an analysis of who is accessing the system, where patient data are stored, where data are shared, and the business uses for the patient data. The analysis must consider both internal users and external users accessing the data from remote locations. Fortunately, there is established guidance for security controls that the project manager may consult. The Health Information Portability and Accountability Act (HIPAA) Security Rule establishes national standards to protect individuals' electronic personal health information that is created, received, used, or maintained by a covered entity. The healthcare organization's security team will require administrative, physical, and technical safeguards to ensure the confidentiality, integrity, and security of electronic PHI.

The privacy team's role is to ensure the confidentiality of the PHI contained in health IT systems. The HIPAA Privacy Rule establishes national standards to protect individuals' medical records and other personal health information. The rule requires appropriate safeguards to protect the privacy of PHI and sets limits and conditions on the uses and disclosures that may be made of such information without patient authorization. These safeguards are largely administrative but are equally important when implementing a health IT system.

Good cybersecurity practices are equally important when implementing these systems for federal agencies such as the National Institutes of Health, Centers for Disease Control and Prevention, and hospitals that serve active-duty military, their dependents, and veterans. Federal agencies are subject to the Privacy Act of 1974 and the Federal Information Security Management

Act (FISMA) of 2002. These acts provide checklists for privacy and security controls for paper and electronic systems maintained by the federal government.

TIP

In 2014, the federal government updated cybersecurity guidance for federal IT systems by giving Department of Homeland Security authority to administer the implementation of information security policies for non-national security federal Executive Branch systems, including providing technical assistance and deploying technologies to such systems.

The system administrator, subject matter experts for the application, the contracting office, and network administrators all have roles to ensure the security and privacy of sensitive data in these systems. Chapter 4 covered risk management and contract management throughout the project. By including all these resources in planning meetings, the project team can identify tasks for security and privacy assessments required by HIPAA and FISMA, conduct testing of implemented security controls and mitigate delays and costly reengineering.

IT Project Security and Privacy Tasks

IT security staff familiar with the hospital's electronic medical record and ancillary IT systems will need to review the new system's technical description, architecture diagrams, data flows, and expected access privileges to make appropriate recommendations for securing the data at rest and in transmission to users and connected IT systems. This may require meetings with the application vendor to discuss options to securely configure servers, encrypt the application, identify security controls for local and remote access to the application, and to plan storage space for auditing, log shipping, and backup recovery systems. The IT security staff will want to know about operating system patching and application updates. Who is going to support the application, and how do they plan to access it? Are any components cloud based? Is the application enabled for mobile devices or Internet access? Each of these is part of a required security risk assessment for HIPAA-covered entities. Even federal government healthcare organizations that are not seeking reimbursement from private insurance or CMS must complete similar security risk assessments to be compliant with FISMA. Project managers must include IT security and privacy staff early in the system planning.

TIP

Project managers must include IT security and privacy staff on the project team and engage them early in the project initiation and planning process groups.

If third parties, such as vendors, will remotely access data for troubleshooting and system support during and after implementation, the security controls at the vendor location and remote access tools used will need to be evaluated by the organization's security staff. Similarly, if the system will share PHI with a third party under contract to perform business operations on behalf of the organization such as billing or coding, the third-party contractor location's security posture must also be evaluated.

What kinds of questions can you expect the security team to ask either of the project or product to be deployed? Below are some of the possible areas that are of interest, because they are raised in almost every single regulatory obligation the security professional needs to adhere to.

- Access management and authentication—if the product cannot be integrated with your company's existing directory services, they will want to know every detail about how accounts will be managed, password complexity and expiration, inactivity timeouts, dormant account policies, and many more.
- Audit and monitoring—HIPAA has rules about logging access to PHI and the length of time you're required to retain those logs. As a result, the security will likely go into depth regarding your system's logging capabilities.
- Protection from malicious code and application security—in addition to network protections, the security team needs to review an application's

ability to withstand attack. Is the vendor's product developed under standard security guidelines? Has it been tested by a third-party evaluator? Is the code digitally signed? Is the system compatible with commercial anti-virus/anti-malware products?

■ Network security—in projects where network security comes into play, the security team will closely scrutinize the requested firewall rules, what the network architecture looks like, how the application presents to the Internet, and what levels of logging are available.

■ Remote access and support—it is standard now that the majority of support for applications and systems is delivered via remote support. The manner in which remote support is obtained will be scrutinized by the security team. Is vendor support "always on," or is it "upon request?" Is it over a secure communications medium? Is access to your internal systems or data restricted to only that which is required for support purposes?

■ Incident response—is always an important topic when it's most needed. What happens when a security event is identified? Have your internal teams been identified, and are they prepared to respond? Are your vendor partners required by contract to notify you within a defined period of time, should they suffer a breach?

■ Configuration management—this is the area where the security team will try to ascertain whether or not the application is running on as secure a platform as possible. They will want to verify the operating system has been hardened against attack, that it is on some sort of patch management program, that vulnerability scans are being performed and the results addressed on a regular basis, and that the product is not running any sort of vulnerable software.

■ Data security—the security team will want to verify that all the relevant data is properly encrypted and using appropriate encryption algorithms. If in a shared or cloud environment, what controls are in place to ensure only your users are able to access your data?

■ Business continuity and disaster recovery—unfortunately, no business can run with the expectation that their systems and data will be available 100% of the time. When your systems or data are partially, or completely unavailable, what is the protocol to ensure the operation continues? Has your business defined their tolerance for system unavailability? Are backup and restoral capabilities part of the project? And will they be tested regularly post-production?

TIP

Testing of remote access to the electronic health record by vendors and third-party contractors should be performed with fictitious data to protect the privacy and confidentiality of the organization's sensitive patient information.

The privacy office will need to execute legally binding documents such as a HIPAA Business Associates Agreement (BAA) or Memorandum of Understanding (MOU) before allowing access to PHI in the production environment. These documents are part of the required privacy risk assessment for HIPAA-covered entities. Their purpose is to record the authorized data uses, data protection requirements, breach notification requirements, and data disposition when the contract ends. The third-party security assessments and agreement on the language in a BAA or MOU can take weeks or months to complete. Each task should be tracked in the work breakdown structure (WBS) and schedule to ensure completion before the system goes live.

The CMS Meaningful Use provisions incentivize organizations to give patients access to their own medical information. If your project includes giving patients access to their medical record via the organization's patient portal or personal health record (PHR), there are a number of tasks that will be added to your project to meet security and privacy requirements. Like most public facing websites, the patient portal or PHR will need to post notice of its privacy practices for patients to read. The privacy notice describes the personal information collected from the website and its intended uses and describes how the organization will secure the patient data made available through the website. Since patients can access the portal website 24/7, the organization will need to share guidance with patients about troubleshooting accounts and access issues that occur outside of business hours. The web application displaying the patient's medical record will be public facing, meaning it is available over the Internet. Public-facing websites are targeted by hackers to gain access to the hospital's IT systems. The security team will ask for an independent vulnerability assessment of the application and require mitigation of identified vulnerabilities before going live. A recommended security practice includes locating these websites in a demilitarized zone that restricts access to the rest of the hospital's network. A proxy will need to be configured to authenticate the patient upon login before reaching behind the hospital's firewall to display only that patient's medical record. The organization's security, privacy, and network team will play a large role in the implementation of patient-facing applications and thus need to be part of the project team.

Department-specific systems, such as those for the laboratory, blood bank, and radiology, are reliant upon medical devices to process patient tests and send those results to the electronic medical record. During the implementation of these systems, the location and security controls of connected medical devices will need to be evaluated. In recent years, hospitals purchasing Food and Drug Administration (FDA)-approved medical devices were reluctant to apply security patches and application updates out of fear that these would negatively impact the function of the device. Many vendors specifically disallow patching these systems, under risk of voiding the warranty or support agreements. Unfortunately, since the medical devices were unpatched, they became the weakest link in the defense of the hospital network from viruses and malware attacks. In 2016, the FDA issued guidance for the selection and management of medical devices, imposing requirements on their manufacturers to test security operating system patches and software application updates against the function of the device and make the patches and updates available to hospitals, providers, and patients using their products. While these new guidelines help remediate the risk, many healthcare facilities already have significant investment in older devices, that have not yet exceeded their useful life, and therefore remain a risk on the network.

TIP

Project managers implementing systems reliant on medical devices may want to consult the FDA for cybersecurity guidance.

It will be important for the project manager to bring the security team and application owners together to plan operations and maintenance for updating the medical devices. Security patches will prevent hackers from being able to take advantage of known vulnerabilities. It will take some time for medical device manufacturers to comply with the guidance. If legacy devices cannot be patched, the security team may propose isolating the devices on an isolated network, or virtual local area network, and other mitigation strategies that will become tasks in the WBS and schedule. If the operating system of the legacy medical device cannot be patched, the network team will work with the security team to segment these devices to minimize risks to the hospital network.

The Office of the National Coordinator for Health Information Technology (ONC) has laid out a 10-year vision for electronic health information exchange (HIE) among hospitals and physician practices participating in state, regional, or community HIE organizations. Electronic health record (EHR) vendors are incorporating the technical requirements and seeking certification of their EHR to allow eligible professionals and hospitals to qualify for CMS Incentive Programs under Meaningful Use. Organizations participating in HIE should have documented data management policies that guide the project manager and project team. The health information management department and privacy office will need to develop patient consents for the exchange of their data and have a plan for obtaining required consents. These tasks will take considerable time and resources to implement and thus should be identified early in the project. Sensitive data or data a patient does not give consent to share must be segmented from the information that is available to the HIE. The vendor implementation specialists and system administrators will need to develop strategies to allow access to basic authorized information and isolate the restricted information. The project management plan should include robust testing of the authentication of HIE participants, the unique patient identifiers, and access to identified data. Corollary tasks will include establishing auditing tools that satisfy HIPAA and FISMA, accounting for disclosure requirements. The security team, system administrator, and network resources will need to work together to develop technical strategies that permit access and the secure flow of data.

TIP

The project team may want to review the toolkits for HIE and interoperability at the HealthIT.gov website for additional guidance.

In an effort to give care providers and patients timely access to the patient medical records, hospitals choose to implement applications on mobile devices such as smart phones, tablets, and laptops. Most EHR vendors already have created mobile-friendly interfaces and provide implementation guidance. The project team will need to consider the management of the care provider's mobile devices to ensure the protection of patient information. Mobile device security requirements include encryption, password protection, authentication to trusted hospital networks, secure local storage of downloaded patient information, and policies for the management of lost or stolen mobile devices. At this phase of the project, the resources should include the security team, network team, system administrator, and local IT support resources. Once the mobile device management is in place, the team will need to test the access and usability of the patient information on the mobile platforms deployed in its organization and solicit input from selected end users. The network team will need to assess the current wireless network and plan for the increased traffic to ensure that it will support timely access and usability of the application and not in a slow, frustrating experience for users.

At the completion of any project, the project manager should require everyone on the project team to update all documentation related to changes made in the system. New hardware, new software, new delivery platforms, and new interconnections with vendors, third parties, and patients can pose additional security risks. A routine post-activation task includes the security team and clinical informatics team updating the organization's documented risk assessments. An organization may have more than one risk assessment. The HHS Security Risk Assessment looks at all of an organization's health IT systems and its security policies and practices. The HIPAA Security Rule recommends that organizations periodically perform analysis of the organization's risk assessment with leadership whenever a significant event occurs, or a major system change is made to the EHR. An organization may also have an ONC Safety Assurance Factors for EHR Resilience (SAFER) self-assessment. The SAFER Guides are designed to help healthcare organizations conduct self-assessments to optimize the safety and safe use of EHRs. Changes in technology and associated healthcare industry practices such as patient portals and HIEs can impact the safety and safe user of the EHR by internal users. Those self-assessments should also be reviewed and updated whenever a major change is made to the EHR. Reminders by the project manager or the configuration management team to the appropriate parties to document changes throughout the project will make it easier to update the risk assessments.

This updated chapter was originally written by Susan M. Martin.

Case Study: Access to System by Outside Resources

Note: This chapter has a unique case study.

Information

Your hospital has decided to shift its scheduling tool to a cloud-based application. Its licensing costs are cheaper than the existing solution and has more functionality. It will require hosting PHI in the cloud-based solution, data feeds between the application and your EHR. Our internal users and your patients will access the tool either via a website or mobile application.

Questions

1. What are the security considerations for hosting PHI in cloud-based tool? What will the access control requirements look like for patient and the hospital user?
2. What are the security and privacy controls at the cloud vendor's IT infrastructure? Will the hospital allow access by an Internet based tool into their EHR? What will need to be considered if the relationship ends?
3. What details are the security team likely to ask you about the solution?
4. How does this modify the Risk Assessment for the hospital?
5. Will you need to develop alternate procedures in the event the Internet, and therefore the tool, are inaccessible?

Feedback

Feedback for this case study can be found in Appendix A.

Chapter 11

Software Testing

> Assumptions aren't facts; they're opportunities for research and testing.

Laurie Buchanan

Testing is one of the most important activities when implementing software of any type. This applies to the initial implementation, as well as the implementation of an upgrade or any change that is completed during operations and maintenance (O&M). In most software projects, there is a testing phase that occurs when the development is completed and before training and the activation or agile release.

TIP

Software testing is a process defined to find errors and verify the system produced the required results.

While this is an important phase of any implementation project, testing should actually occur throughout the project in one form or another. However, most of the test effort occurs after the requirements have been defined and the development has been completed. The software development methodology that is chosen leads into the definition of the testing methodology. The design needs to be carefully checked against requirements prior to any development to ensure that it meets the customer's needs and expectations.

DOI: 10.4324/9781003206668-11

Unit testing occurs during development to verify each piece of code or configuration prior to release to the test team. During the project planning phase, the test plan defines what type of testing will be completed, what materials will be developed, and the expectations of the test team. Expected deliverables from the testing phase include test scripts, test scenarios, test reports, test plans, and how test incidents will be reported and managed.

TIP

The National Institute of Standards and Technology (2010) report notes that catching software "bugs" before a system is released enhances security from hacker exploitation. As cybersecurity becomes more important over the years, testing is being expanded beyond validating just a system's functionality.

The concept of software bugs is related more to custom software development projects as opposed to the implementation of a commercial off-the-shelf (COTS) product, but there are times when customers find bugs in COTS software and report them to the vendor.

Organizations that develop software or support software systems often have a specific person or team who focuses on testing. Those doing testing need to understand the requirements from specific functionality to workflows, or how the system will be used. They also need to be aware of the dataflows, or how data will flow through integration with other systems, or within the system itself.

The training testers on how to use the system should occur as early as possible in the project schedule. The test team should review the requirements in detail to ensure they will all be included in the testing process, either through detailed test scripts or in broader testing scenarios. Testers should also meet with users to ensure that their workflows are addressed in the process. These activities help the testers develop the scripts, scenarios, and the expected outcomes for each.

There are a variety of testing types that are possible for software projects. How much testing and what types are needed for individual projects are highly dependent on the project itself and the amount of time available for testing. The organization's tolerance for risk and the defined risk mitigation strategies also will influence the plans for testing, as well as the organizational sensitivity and impact of the project. The more testing, the less risk, but there are usually constraints impacting the available time or resources for this activity. It is often a well-balanced approach that works best.

A project related to pediatric medication dosing will have more stringent testing requirements than one related to outpatient clinic scheduling. Both are very important to the organization and need to be done correctly, but one impacts patient safety while the other impacts patient and clinic inconvenience. Below are brief descriptions of different testing types and when they might be used in a software implementation project.

Testing Types

Unit testing is the testing of individual software components to ensure that they function as designed without generating unexpected errors prior to integration with other components. Generally, this testing is completed during the software's development and includes items such as checking the spelling of displayed items, ensuring they are in the correct location on the system screen, and checking that data is saved as expected. This concept also applies to COTS systems, in which the software is configured to meet the organization's processes. If, for example, there is an option of what happens when the user double clicks on a patient name in the patient list, does the expected result occur? Unit testing is also applicable for any ongoing changes made to the system during operations and maintenance. This is also called "component testing" and is the only type of testing with which the developers should be involved.

Once development is complete, the code is moved to a dedicated test environment where all changes are controlled to minimize the impact to the ongoing testing processes. For smaller systems, testing may occur in a combined development/test environment. In this environment, functional testing is conducted to determine that the integrated components function as designed.

Functional testing is completed by the testing staff and is based on the functional requirements. Defined test scripts are used to perform functional testing; each script is written to verify a specific requirement or a group of requirements. A sample test script is in Table 11.1. Besides testing how the integrated components function, based on the requirements, functional testing ensures that the code follows the organizations business processes. This includes a series of tests using normal and erroneous data that should mimic what real users would enter.

Table 11.1   Portion of Sample Test Script

#	Task	Data	Expected Outcome	P/F	Comment
1	Enter URL	<URL to be opened>	Website appears with logo in top right corner, login/password fields and privacy verbiage at the bottom	P	
2	Enter login/password and select "Enter"	Login=testrn; PW=testrn	The home screen of the application appears and displays…	F	Received the error "error verbiage documented here"
3					

Testing the integration or connection between multiple modules, multiple systems, or portions of a single system is called *system integration testing.* This is used for testing the applied business process scenarios in conjunction with the components and interfaces to ensure that the system as a whole is functioning correctly. This testing is based on business scenarios to demonstrate how the modules, or systems, work together and verify the data flows as expected. For example, if an order is entered for a chest x-ray, did the order cross the interface and does it appear in the radiology system? If expected, did the order requisition print in the radiology department or in the patient care unit? If you have a single sign-on solution and change your password, can you continue to access each system with the new password?

System integration testing is full testing of the system with a focus on the big picture. This testing verifies the system connections between any external or third-party systems defined in the system requirements. The test of a process, from beginning to end, is completed within scenarios rather than within detailed test scripts. One example would be to admit a patient to the hospital and enter a variety of orders that would be sent to a number of different systems. Testing would include verifying whether the order went to the ancillary system as expected through an interface message or that a requisition that prints. If a result is entered, will it come back to the original system for the patient care staff to view? Are any medication orders available for the nursing staff to document against? This testing is completed in the test environment or in the preproduction environment of each system being tested by the team.

Once a system has been tested, any modifications such as resolution of issues or new requested changes should be followed by regression testing. If development is completed in phases, this would include the introduction of each additional phase. If regression testing is expected during the project, it should be included in the test plan and project schedule. *Regression testing* is a method of verifying that a new change does not break another part of the system's functionality that has already been in place. This should be completed on its own. Standard regression test scripts are developed to be followed each time a change is introduced and include a variety of basic features to ensure that the system functionality is preserved without any negative impact. Similar in scope to a functional test, a regression test allows a consistent, repeatable validation of each component of the system after new change. While regression testing can be performed manually, an automated tool is often used to reduce the time and resources needed to perform this repeatable testing.

When developing custom systems, it is important to test the system's compatibility with different workstation configurations. This includes different operating systems and hardware platforms. This type of testing is called *non-functional testing*. Are there specific minimum requirements for the amount of memory or operating system versions? Do the requirements define which browsers the system should work with? If not, this type of testing would help define the minimum requirements needed to run the system. Non-functional testing is also used for validation of different types of workstations, such as virtual or thin clients.

Vendors will provide the minimum requirements necessary for their systems when you purchase them. This testing is repeated as technology changes to verify that the system remains compatible with the latest versions and can be completed manually or through an automated tool.

Performance testing—also called load testing or stress testing—is completed in an environment that closely resembles production. This testing helps the technical staff, both in understanding the scalability of the system and to create a benchmark of the performance of new hardware. It is useful in the identification of any bottlenecks for high-use systems and is generally completed through the use of automated tools that can mimic peak-load conditions. It is also important to understand the accessibility of the system from the different workstations located throughout the organization.

This would include understanding the performance of a wireless network. How many workstations will be located in a single location and how will that impact available bandwidth? Are there any dead zones where the wireless network is unavailable, and is this acceptable? This will be key if users will be accessing the system from portable or mobile devices. The wireless network may need to be expanded if it is unavailable where the users will need access.

User acceptance testing obtains confirmation by the business subject matter experts (SMEs), preferably the owner or super users from the business community, on the usability and match of the software to mutually agreed upon requirements. This testing is scenario based, such as a list of activities to complete rather than using detailed test scripts which list each specific step. For example, a scenario would have the following tasks listed: (1) login, (2) find Patient <provide test patient name>, (3) enter an initial assessment. The tester is not given specific instructions. This will require them to receive training on the system prior to performing this testing.

One example of a scenario-based test is that of a new patient who has arrived in the emergency department (ED). The nurse performs his or her normal activities but utilizes the new system rather than the organization's current paper-based process or legacy system. The test is scheduled and runs in a controlled environment, and the work is completed in the test or preproduction environments. The scenario may identify all possible activities, even optional ones, to ensure all are validated. Be prepared to receive a lot of feedback from the users who are conducting this testing. This is likely the first time they have seen the system, and each will have opinions on how it is working and suggested improvements.

Every item should be documented, evaluated, and categorized based on feedback or action items. Critical issues should be resolved before the end of the testing phase, allowing for retesting prior to moving forward. Education issues should be provided to the training team to be incorporated in the training and possibly included in a frequently asked questions (FAQs) document that can be reviewed by users prior to the activation. Some issues might need to be provided to the business owners for evaluation if they relate to the new workflows or processes. Enhancements, or new requirements, can be reviewed and added to the scope of this project, or deferred to after the system is live in the next phase, or as part of O&M processes. Categorizing the feedback will help the team focus on what needs to be resolved right away and plan for the others.

Parallel testing is similar to user acceptance testing, but the staff are doing their work using the current processes plus the new electronic process in parallel. This requires additional staff and is completed while in the work environment. For example, when the patient arrives to be admitted, one admission clerk would admit the patient using the current paper/electronic process while another takes the same information and enters it into the new admission system. This provides more realistic evaluation of the business fit and workflows but it does require additional staffing and access to the system from the admissions department.

Cybersecurity testing is a newer type of testing that should be completed prior to bringing the system live and repeated at a regular interval during operations and maintenance. This testing validates the security of the system from hackers, malware, viruses, or other outside threats. The organization's security team usually facilitates this process and may work with an independent organization that specializes in this type of testing. The validation of the access control policy, network penetration tests, or vulnerability scans are just a few of these types of tests. The intent is to identify any potential security issues early and resolve them prior to any external threats. Most organizations require this testing, and the resolution of any critical issues, to be completed prior to the system going live to minimize risks.

As mentioned earlier, the level of testing is dependent on the uniqueness, complexity, and impact of the software being implemented. A small, simple system might only include a few types of testing, while the larger, more complex systems would lend themselves to more. There is no right or wrong answer on when to perform each type or whether some can be completed concurrently, such as combining function and integration testing.

Configuration and Release Management

Configuration management is the discipline of controlling configuration items throughout the system's lifecycle. Configuration items are any single entity that can be uniquely identified. This includes portions of software code, systems settings, hardware configuration, or system documentation. Items can vary widely in complexity and size, ranging from a single software setting to an entire system.

Configuration management includes identifying, documenting, tracking, coordinating, and controlling the current status of these items, their versions, and relationships. The goal of configuration management is to ensure the integrity of the software and hardware. Strong configuration management imposes control over activities that are often unmanageable and complex.

The configuration management plan documents how this process will be integrated into an organization. The plan often includes definition of need, any policies or procedures, responsibilities, and defined processes. It is important to identify what configuration items will be under configuration management, what information about the items will be tracked, and what process a requested change goes through before being implemented into production. For example, you may not need to document or track the request to add a new user, but the request to update a pharmacy order should require steps to ensure approval from the impacted departments and possibly the patient care committee. The second example may also require some analysis, tracking of the change through the various environments, full testing, and communication to the pharmacy and care givers.

Tools are available to assist with automating parts of the process and can provide a method of documenting the baseline of each configurable item, as well as providing version control when modifications are approved.

TIP

Under configuration management, each change should be fully tested prior to migrating the change into the production environment.

All project managers are familiar with change management. The importance of managing changes to software and hardware is as important as managing changes to the project scope or requirements. The concepts are the same. This is a formal process to control and coordinate all changes to a production system and includes how changes are requested, prioritized, and approved. A Change Control Board often undertakes these processes and includes key stakeholders, as well as system and information technology (IT) SMEs. They have the authority to approve or deny requested changes based on analysis and recommendations.

Once approved, each change should be fully tested and scheduled prior to being migrated to production. This should be a repeatable process that is fully documented and communicated. The different environments that are available for the specific system will define the steps of this process. Will there be separate development and test environments or one environment for both activities? See Chapter 9 for a discussion on environments. The process includes how changes are made and migrated through the different available environments and when they will be tested or validated.

Release management refers to the activities surrounding the release of a specific version of the system. Changes should be introduced into an environment on a controlled schedule. This will reduce the impact to the users and allows for a single regression testing event per release. Migrating changes to the test environment on a set schedule allows the testing staff to know exactly what needs to be tested and provides a stable location to test without constant changes that could impact the results. Packaging the changes into a scheduled release for production ensures that they are migrated in a controlled manner. Only those that passed testing are included and limits when changes occur that might impact the end users.

When implementing software, configuration management would begin as soon as a configurable item is identified, and baseline information is collected. For software development, this would begin when a piece of code is completed and placed under version control. For a COTS implementation, this might be as soon as the configuration is complete.

In either case, configuration management begins prior to the main testing activities. Once the testing activities are completed, the system should be considered frozen until activation. This will ensure that there is time to fully test all modifications and reduce the risk of last-minute changes having a negative impact on production.

Case Study 1: Implementation of an Electronic Health Record

Type: COTS

Additional Information

You have been informed that a group of super users has been identified to assist with the project. They are a combination of nurses and physicians who represent the different patient care areas. They have been involved in redesigning the workflows and developing the requirements. It took a long time to obtain agreement on how the new features' will be configured. The IT and vendor staff are now busy with development based on the requirements.

Questions

1. How could you utilize the super users during testing?
2. What types of testing would you include with this project/program?
3. What types of items would be placed under configuration management?

Feedback

Feedback for this case study can be found in Appendix A.

Case Study 2: Implementation of an Organizational Metrics Dashboard

Type: Custom development

Additional Information

You have been informed that a group of super users has been identified to assist with the project. They have been involved in developing the requirements for the new system and are familiar with all data to be collected.

Questions

1. How could you utilize the super users during testing?
2. What types of testing would you include with this project/program?
3. What types of items would be placed under configuration management?

Feedback

Feedback for this case study can be found in Appendix A.

Chapter 12

Activation Management

> Talent wins games, but teamwork and intelligence win championships.
>
> **Michael Jordan**

Planning for software activation begins during project initiation and continues through planning, execution, and controlling. Decisions made during these process groups feed into the implementation strategy and how the software will be activated. With the project team's focus on system design, development, and testing, actual planning for activation can be forgotten until it is too late.

This chapter will review what it takes to have a successful activation, beginning with initial planning through the post-live support of end users. Training also will be included, since this activity occurs right before the go-live and is a key step to ensuring that everyone ready to begin using the new software when it is available. When the software is not ready or the users are unprepared, the initial perceptions will be negative, and these are not easy to change.

TIP

There are a variety of definitions available for what activation planning means. For the purpose of this book, activation planning will be defined as the activities and planning surrounding the go-live or activation of a software system.

DOI: 10.4324/9781003206668-12

User Training

A training plan should be part of the project management plan, and it should outline how training will be accomplished and when. The size and scope of the project will define the type of training required. For the more complex project, the most common options are a trainer-led classroom, online computer-based training (CBT), or a combination of the two. For a project with minimal changes for the end users, communication with a tip sheet outlining the changes, or frequently asked questions (FAQs) that include responses to each, may be sufficient.

If a combination plan were used, one option would be to have the basic functionality included in the CBT, followed by classroom training that includes the more advanced features. Having multiple CBTs of short duration allows users to complete them during breaks in their normal work hours. Trainer-led classroom training will require staff to be away from their normal workplace.

The training staff should utilize the requirements and design documentation to help plan what training materials will be required. The training should include the functionality of the new software, as well as any changes in workflow or processes to ensure the users are fully prepared to use the system right after activation.

The quantity and type of courses will depend on the user population. Will different groups of users have access to different functionality? Do they need to be trained differently because of their security access? Will physicians, nurses, pharmacists, and respiratory therapists all require the same level of training? Understanding the different groups of users, what system functionality they will be using, and the level of security for the software will help make these decisions.

Oftentimes, the development of the training material has to wait until the software is available to the training team. This typically follows the development or configuration phase of the project. Depending on the development strategy, they might have access to functionality at various times throughout the project, if it is being completed in phases or through an iterative process.

Training should occur as close to the activation date as possible, so the students do not forget what they have learned. When there are 50 to 100 users, this might not be an issue, but when implementing a system with 3,000 users, it can be more challenging. When training must start earlier than desired to ensure all have the opportunity to attend, the training plan should include ways to help the attendees to remember what was taught. These could include tip sheets, FAQs, as with smaller projects, and post-live support that includes hands on guidance as they begin to use the new system.

The staff 's normal work hours should be taken into consideration when scheduling training. Will classes be offered on the evening and night shift in a hospital setting? If training staff in a physician's practice, will the office schedule be kept clear of patient appointments or will training occur after-hours?

Another consideration is whether the training will be mandatory. If it is, there needs to be consequences for those not attending, such as not receiving their access to the software until after they attend. While this ensures that all users have completed training, it could cause disruption if staff are scheduled to work after the activation, but do not have access.

If there is a large group of people who need to be trained, one or more training rooms should be set up to allow the maximum number of students to be trained over the shortest period of time. This would require additional trainers and access to additional workstations if the attendees will be expected to access the system for any practice exercises. Since it is important to keep classroom size small enough for optimal learning, multiple classrooms would be beneficial.

In many cases, the workstations in the training rooms are provided with specific training patients and training user accounts. This allows students to have access to their own unique patient with the correct security access so they are learning with the same access they will have when the system is live. The patients will have specific data preloaded to coincide with the training materials. One example is when students are shown how to look up a patient's allergies; there should be allergies present for them to find. Having medication orders already in place is beneficial for nurses to learn how to document the medication administration.

If user acceptance testing or parallel testing is included in the implementation strategy, any feedback that is training specific should be brought to the training team as soon as possible. Modifying the training materials, or at least verbally going over these items, will help to better prepare the users.

Training is one of the key elements that can make the project successful. This is often the first time any of the users have seen the software, and first impressions tend to last a long time. Proper planning and execution are critical, along with the efforts of a dedicated training team. Since these activities coincide with planning for the actual activation activities; having a strong lead of the training team helps the project manager keep both activities on schedule.

Activation

As mentioned previously, activation planning should begin as early as possible in the project's lifecycle. The larger and more complex the project, the sooner this planning should begin. A general guide used by some is two to four months prior to activation for medium-sized projects and four to six months for large or complex projects.

TIP

As a general rule of thumb, detailed activation planning should begin approximately two months prior to the activation of a smaller project. A larger, more complex, project could require four to six months.

Another factor that impacts the amount of activation planning required is the activation strategy. Will the users be moving from paper to electronic? Is there a legacy system in place, requiring data migration prior to the use of the new software? Will the new software be rolled out one area at a time, or one function at a time? Will one area be a pilot, and if all goes well, be rolled out to all others at the same time? Answers to these questions will help you define the planning and activities needed to move forward.

Any decisions that were made early in the project should be considered when this planning begins. This will help identify what decisions are remaining to be made. Each decision will have a downstream impact on the activities to follow. The use of an options document will help compare each available option and provide the level of detail needed for an educated decision.

An options document includes a description of the decision to be made and a description of each option. The document also includes the advantages, disadvantages, and other key information, such as resources required and costs, all of which should be presented in a table to allow for easy comparison. The options could be the columns with the different types of information in rows. With this format, the rows should always include a description, pros or advantages, cons or disadvantages, constraints, and assumptions. The rest of the rows will depend on the decision to be made. The additional rows should include all information of importance to differentiate the options being evaluated. Some potential information to include are listed below.

- Impact to workflows
- Impact to dataflows
- Budget or cost to implement
- Budget or cost for ongoing support
- Required resources
- Duration or timeline
- Risks
- Required hardware
- Technical impact
- Business impact
- User impact
- Ongoing support impact
- Other (general category)

The team putting the document together should provide a recommendation and justification for the option they selected. While there seems to be a lot of information included, it is important to keep it simple, factual, and objective. The final decision makers are the project sponsors or executive sponsors. They may choose to include others in the discussions, but they are accountable for the final decision.

One major decision for any activation is the actual date and time to begin the go-live activity. This might seem simple but depending on the number of staff required and duration of the activity, along with post-live support, it can be a real challenge. Variables to consider include holidays, school calendars for staff's children, vacations, historically high census periods, and organizational activities, such as accreditation visits. The impact on end users also should be considered, especially when extra staffing is planned to help once the new system is live. Additional decisions would involve how to ensure the right data are available when needed.

If implementing an electronic medical record (EMR), how will the patients, the active medical orders for the current inpatients, or the schedules for the outpatients be entered so they are available when the users begin utilizing the system? What results will be entered or loaded? Will past laboratory or radiology results be loaded? If so, how far back? Some decisions are necessary early in the planning stage, while others will continue to be identified as the planning continues.

As with project management, communication is one of the most important aspects of activation planning. This includes communication to all stakeholders, such as the end users, organizational leadership, and the project team. Once a decision is made on the date and time of the activation, this should be communicated, so the departments can begin their preparations. Managers need time to schedule the appropriate staff, since their schedules can be created six to eight weeks in advance.

As additional decisions are made and more information is gathered, you should have as your goal the kind of communication that arrives early and often and is clear and concise. This can be challenging as staff may not always read their e-mails or remember what they read. A variety of communication methods should be used, such as flyers, posters, and attending their staff meetings. Be creative in getting the message out. Remember to also communicate any changes to these plans if the activation date or time slips. Stakeholder management and communications are also discussed in Chapter 8.

TIP

It is not uncommon to hear an end user say, "I didn't know about this."

Activation Checklist

Identification of the specific tasks that are required to activate the new software is an essential step to preparation. There are a variety of different ways to facilitate the identification and documentation these tasks, but this book will describe one—an activation checklist. This checklist provides a very detailed look at all tasks required surrounding the actual go-live.

The checklist is a detailed list of all tasks that occur before, during, and after go-live. It is similar to a work plan, but with a more comprehensive list of tasks. The level of detail can be found all the way down to tasks with durations of only minutes. The development of the checklist begins with a face-to-face meeting of all staff involved.

During this meeting, tasks are identified and then placed in sequence. An easy—and low-tech—way of accomplishing this is with the aid of sticky notes. (You could do this electronically, but many prefer the sticky notes because they tend to be a bit more interactive). Each person at the meeting writes one task per sticky note and includes the resource and estimated duration. Once all tasks are collected, they are sorted by the order in which they should occur or if multiple tasks can be completed simultaneously. These meetings provoke a lot of discussion, and a task identified by one person often triggers thoughts of others that should be included.

After this meeting, the tasks, durations, estimated start and finish times, resources, and comments are entered into a spreadsheet. Remember to think of this checklist as a living document, something that will change each time it is reviewed, and more information is obtained. Regular meetings should be scheduled to review the checklist with the goal of having a complete list of all required tasks. If this is a lengthy activation with many tasks, or the staff are new to this process, it might take multiple meetings to get through the first draft. This iterative process helps to verify that the right tasks are identified, in the right order, with the right predecessors, and assigned to the right resources.

Subsequent meetings often include some good discussion about what should happen, how, and when. These are often important topics to get through, even if they appear to take the meeting off topic. Through these discussions, it may be identified that additional tasks can be completed concurrently, which saves more time. While the process is sometimes tedious, not having a checklist or having an incomplete one will lead to missing tasks, tasks performed out of order requiring rework, team frustration, or an extended downtime. These all lead to increased risks and unhappy users.

As the team reviews the checklist, they should be asked what could go wrong during each task. Discussing and planning for the worst will provide a response strategy to be documented in advance, rather than trying to come up with a plan on the fly when the situation arises. This provides a level of contingency planning, which is very beneficial on activation day since it rarely goes as planned.

The contingency plan should include how to completely roll back to the previous version, or system, if a severe issue cannot be resolved. Some questions to ask: how would tasks be undone if needed? Where should go/no-go decisions be placed in the checklist, and who has the authority to make these decisions? The entire team present during the activation should be involved in the go/no-go discussion, but the project manager must make sure the decision maker is available when needed, if they are not present during the entire activity.

Activation Rehearsal

Once the project manager and team feel that the checklist is complete, the next step is a test by conducting an activation rehearsal. Running a full rehearsal of the planned activity will help validate the checklist related to tasks and their duration and order, as well as help to identify anything that is missing. This also provides a practice for any tasks that might be new to the technical staff. This should be as close to the actual activation as possible, and a copy of production should be used to best understand the actual tasks and durations.

For the rehearsal, as well as the activation, it is best if everyone is located in the same space to ensure proper communication, collaboration, and coordination. A person should be assigned to run the checklist, which means he or she coordinates what activities are happening, documenting actual start and end time, any comments or issues. As these occur, the checklist will be updated with new identified tasks, modifications to the order of tasks and resolution for issues.

The project manager should be free to troubleshoot issues, communicate with others, and assist where needed. The resources assigned to each task need to notify the checklist coordinator when they begin and end each task, as well as if there are any changes to the tasks themselves. This ensures that everything is correctly documented. Nothing should be deleted from the checklist; using strikethrough and a different color of font, helps to identify changes since the final checklist becomes a key document when preparing for the actual activation.

After the rehearsal, a lessons-learned meeting should be held. This meeting should be used to review the rehearsal event and what changes are necessary for the real activation. The checklist is reviewed and modified based on the updates made during the rehearsal. This includes modifying the durations, order of tasks, or the tasks themselves. Any issues should be evaluated for how best to avoid them and the contingency plan should be updated based on the resolution. This helps with decreasing risks and delays while trying to find the resolution when it is known.

Other lessons could involve communication, amount and type of staff needed for the activity, the timing of when staff is needed for assigned tasks, and the overall duration of the activity, including the duration of any system downtime. The rehearsal is the time to make mistakes, and if it went very poorly or major modifications to the checklist were required, take the time to repeat the rehearsal prior to the actual activation. Don't worry about a rehearsal that went poorly, rather think of it as a lesson and an opportunity to improve prior to the actual activation.

Things to consider for the activation:

- Do you have a location large enough for the entire team?
- Are there enough computers for the entire team? Do they have laptops?
- Are there enough network ports, power outlets?
- Is there a phone available for a conference call for others to check in? Is it in a location in which everyone can hear and be heard and not on a wall or in a corner of the room?
- If some resources are remote, such as vendor staff, do they have the necessary access to what they need?
- Is there a way to display the checklist in real-time, as it is being updated, so all can see the most current version?
- Do you have a way to stay in contact with staff outside of the room using radios or cell phones?
- Do you need to provide food and drink for the staff? Is the cafeteria open during the activation window? Will people have time to leave to get food?
- Do you have a mode of communication for users to request assistance? Is this needed during the downtime or will it begin after everything is live?
- Will you have staff making rounds throughout the facility to provide status updates, answer questions, or just-in-time training? When will this occur, the last few hours prior to the system being live and after?
- If all staff are remote, what is the best way to ensure proper collaboration and communication?

During the final weeks of activation planning, last-minute fixes and training will be going on. It is important to institute a system freeze prior to the activation to ensure that there is time to fully test all modifications and so everyone can feel confident that the system is stable and ready for the activation. This should be at least one week prior to go-live, but two weeks is better. Making changes at the last minute is very risky, with limited time to completely test the change and any potential downstream affects. Sometimes, it is necessary to make a last-minute change. The approval for these last-minute changes should be made by the project sponsor or executive sponsors with careful considerations of the constraints and risks.

During these final weeks, communication will continue throughout the organization to ensure that all are well informed about the upcoming activity. If there is a current electronic system that will be unavailable during the activation, the project manager should check to see if any hardcopy reports are necessary to support work processes or patient care during the downtime and include a task of printing the reports when they are needed. If a read-only version is available, the work to make it available should be added to the checklist.

All of the planning and preparations have led up to the day of the actual activation. The project team is aware of what is expected of them, when they need to be onsite, and what tasks they will be doing. The users know what to expect, whether there is a downtime or not. They have been trained and understand their new workflows and processes as well as the downtime processes. However, despite all the work to refine and finalize the checklist and plan for any contingencies, something will come up that was not anticipated. Adding buffer tasks to the checklists, maybe in conjunction with the go/no-go decisions, will provide time to work past these unexpected surprises.

TIP

Adding buffer tasks to the checklist provides extra time for any unexpected delays. If all goes well, the system will go live earlier than expected.

Building in plenty of time to complete system and regression testing prior to allowing users into the system will allow the team to resolve any issues that may arise during the testing. With proper planning, the right people will be available, either in the room or by phone, to resolve any issues that come up.

Once the system is live, post-live support begins. This activity involves both the technical and clinical staff. Good planning is necessary for a smooth transition to the new software and work processes. Users will need help, whether it is in answering questions about how to do something or in resolving an issue that needs fixing. Support staff should be ready to respond when needed.

A Help Desk or hotline should be shared prior to the activation. Flyers posted on workstations also can help. Scheduling support staff will ensure that they are available during the user's business hours for a period of time after the activation. Users appreciate having them making rounds and providing guidance and just-in-time training. Even with the staff making rounds, there will still be a need for staff answering the hotline phone. For some systems, this period of support may only be necessary for a few days, while larger implementations might require support for weeks. The support should span the work hours of the users, which may vary between a hospital, which is 24 × 7, or a physician's practice, which will have shorter work hours. If a help desk is already in place, staffing may need to be enhanced right after the activation in anticipation of additional calls. They should also receive communication on what issues may be reported, how they can be resolved, or who to assign the help desk ticket to. These are further defined in Chapter 13.

Users also will want to make modifications to the software; however, it is important that users become familiar with the software and the new processes prior to making suggestions for modifications. The requests should be to improve the system and not to just make it the same as what they had before. Of course, this does not include critical issues or patient safety concerns, which should be resolved right away. Users should understand the process of requesting future enhancements, as well as how they are approved and prioritized.

Activation planning is a complex activity and includes several components. It requires a very detail-oriented person to help move the team through this lengthy process. With proper planning, the software will be successfully activated, and the end users will be well prepared. Detailed documentation and clear concise communication are two of the key elements of proper activation planning. Having all steps and configuration settings documented ahead of time ensures that the settings that were tested are the settings being implemented. This documentation also allows for other staff to step in and complete the task, if necessary. Remember, it is okay to make mistakes in the rehearsal as long as you learn from them for the activation.

Case Study 1: Implementation of an Electronic Health Record

Type: Commercial off-the-shelf

Additional Information

The activation strategy decision is to go-live with all new functionality in a Big Bang. This will include users in all patient care areas.

Questions

1. What main activities would occur during the activation?
2. What level of post-live support should be scheduled?

Feedback

Feedback for this case study can be found in Appendix A.

Case Study 2: Implementation of a Research Tracking System

Type: Custom development

Additional Information

The activation strategy decision is to go-live with all functionality in a Big Bang. This will include all identified users. It has been requested that the historical data be loaded into the new system.

Questions

1. What main activities would occur during the activation?
2. How would the activation change if this project was managed using an Agile method?
3. What level of post-live support should be scheduled?

Feedback

Feedback for this case study can be found in Appendix A.

Chapter 13

Project Transition to Support

Ryan D. Kennedy

> Look on every exit as being an entrance somewhere else.
>
> **Tom Stoppard**

One of the measures of success for any industry is the opportunity to take on additional and more complex responsibilities. For a project management office (PMO), this is showcased through the assignment of new projects with longer durations, higher risk, larger budgets, and greater numbers of resources. As the number of active projects grows, it becomes imperative for the PMO to implement a methodology that will allow for the successful transition of closed projects to operational and support staff.

The importance of a smooth transition process cannot be overstated. Even if you have the best project manager (PM) assigned to the project, who meticulously managed a project through a successful go-live that was on-time, on-budget, and within scope, none of that will matter if the customer cannot get the support they need when they need it. The PM needs to consider not just the success of the project, but also the long-term success of the product or service. One does not equal the other. These are two very different mindsets that are also intimately intertwined.

Since most PMs would never want to see their product fail, even after the project is complete, they will do what they can to keep the customer satisfied, even if that means becoming the de facto support person. This is clearly not an optimal situation, and PMs will find themselves spending too much of their time supporting the products and services of past projects, rather than focusing their efforts on bringing new and exciting changes to the organization.

DOI: 10.4324/9781003206668-13

Why Does This Happen?

As we learned early in this book, the core definition of a project is that they are temporary, with a defined beginning and end. Once a project is closed, PMs should be able to distance themselves from the scope of that work and, in particular, the support and maintenance that are necessary to keep the product or service operational. This is not easily accomplished, even in offices that have a well-defined transition plan. Throughout the project, the PM is the one resource who was involved from beginning to end and likely understands the nuances of the product that was implemented: he or she was responsible for tracking risks and resolving issues; he or she ensured that all project personnel had the resources necessary to complete their work; and the PM likely developed a constructive rapport with stakeholders, customers, and sponsors. While these elements describe the traits of a great PM, they also contribute to a potentially dangerous reputation that the PM is the only person that can facilitate, prioritize, and escalate issues as they come up after the project is complete.

Imagine this scenario: you are the sponsor of a project that will result in the deployment of a new software application for your team. You expect that this application will serve a critical role in the mission of your organization and will therefore need to be accessible 24/7. At the end of the project, your strong PM informs you that she will be stepping aside but assures you that the organization's support center will be able to handle any future concerns quickly and efficiently. The first time an issue is encountered, you will likely take the advice of the PM and work through the defined support center. However, if you find that any aspect of that process is less optimal than the customer service you experienced during the project, you may find yourself reaching back out to the PM for alternative options or for escalation for faster resolution.

The PM is now in a no-win situation: if the PM declines to intervene, he or she risks breaking the professional relationship that was developed during the project, not to mention the perception that he or she is not providing the type of customer service that his or her organization may be expecting. If the PM does intervene, it will illegitimatize the services of the support center and devalue their staff. Likewise, the PM will continue to be called upon for future issues, which will take away from his or her availability for the other projects he or she is already assigned.

In the rest of this chapter, we will identify how to create a successful project handoff to avoid this situation in the first place. We will also explore how to respond to requests for future services in a way that will not damage professional relationships and build upon customer service skills.

TIP

A successful transition to support enables the project manager to move on to other projects while maintaining a positive customer service experience.

One characteristic that defines all of us as humans is that we are lazy. By that, we always look to find the path of least resistance to accomplish our goals. Therefore, it becomes evident that to have a successful handoff, you must have a support structure that is just as, if not more, efficient than working through the PM directly. Otherwise, customers will always go back to the PM, who had traditionally been responsive and friendly with routine communication and follow-up. Therefore, it's important to take a moment to explore the characteristics of a successful support center. From this list, we can define a transition process that will complement those traits.

Characteristics of a Support Center

There are an abundance of references that can be used to develop a customer support center, so to condense that into a few paragraphs for the purposes of this chapter, we will need to make a few assumptions about the existing environment. First, staff should be allocated and available to provide operational support to existing systems. This may be a mix of dedicated staff or product managers, as well as staff who alternate between operational support and new project activities. There should already be a central reference point for customers to turn to, such as a help desk number or an electronic ticketing system. And finally, we will assume that customers are at least generally aware of the existing support center and have a generally favorable view of it. Of course, creating a generally favorable perception of a support center can be challenging (how would you rate your interactions with your cable or phone provider's call center?), but there are some strategies that can be implemented to make this experience as productive as possible.

1. *Strive for first call resolution*—it can be infuriating to customers when they are continually relayed from person to person and having to re-explain their issue several times. The support center should be equipped with enough information to be able to respond to as many issues as possible on the customer's first contact with the center.
2. *Include an escalation process*—although it would be phenomenal for every issue to be resolved on first contact, the reality is that certain subject matter experts will need to be involved. These individuals should be well aware of their role in the support process, as well as their tier level (at what point they are contacted). Likewise, they need to have a good understanding of the product or service with an issue, or at least a clear method of finding that information quickly.
3. *Ensure that resources meet demands*—this includes resources at all tier levels, so customers experience minimal wait times when calling the first time and minimal resolution times when cases do need to be escalated to higher-level tiers in the organization. Compiling metrics of hold times and open ticket durations can help identify areas of concern.
4. *Compile metrics on frequent issues*—if multiple users are contacting the support center with the same common questions or concerns, perhaps the situation needs to be addressed at a more global level. Keeping track of these issues, much like a PM would do on a project, can help discover trends early.
5. *Create an environment of positive customer support*—customers can tell if they are the 3rd or the 300th issue or call the representative has had to deal with that day. Remind frontline staff that they are the face of the organization or the product, and keeping a positive demeanor is critical to success. This applies internally, as well: disgruntled workers with a grudge against other team members should never vocalize those concerns to the customer. Internal issues should be dealt with internally and immediately at a supervisor-to-employee level, as the various tiers of support need to work with each other just as much as they need to work with the customer.
6. *Ensure that every product has an owner*—when all else fails, there needs to be someone who is ultimately responsible for the operations of the product or service. As tempting as it may be, that individual should never be the PM. This is an excellent opportunity to appoint a *product* manager for this purpose, or at least someone who can function in a similar role, such as a business owner or an application

administrator. This person will be a key member of the transition team as we start to explore the role of the PM in transitioning projects to products.

Change Management

What happens when a request for service is beyond the break/fix phase and requires major enhancements or improvements? In addition to a strong support center, an organization needs to have a process in place to handle changes to a system after related projects are closed. It's useful to group post-live system changes into two distinct categories: (1) maintenance and (2) project.

Changes that would be considered general maintenance could include modifications that require a low number of resources, funding, or level of effort. Groups of changes can be combined together for a streamlined and organized implementation in scheduled release cycles using a well-defined process known as change management or configuration management. Using this strategy, the previous PM should not have any role in the ongoing modifications of the system. This is facilitated by a product manager, oftentimes in conjunction with stakeholders, developers, testers, and a configuration management team. Change management was discussed in more detail in Chapter 11.

If the changes being requested take substantial work effort or funding, they could be rolled up into a new project altogether. Organizations can create their own definition as to what is considered maintenance and what is considered a project but having that distinction can help set appropriate expectations for all impacted parties. For example, if a change request to a software application requires a major upgrade and new hardware, resources from the information technology (IT) team may not be immediately available to respond to the need. Therefore, a project request governance process can be implemented that involves committees and stakeholders in a consolidated effort to determine the appropriate priorities for all major work across the organization. Once approved to start, a new PM can be assigned to start the project management cycle over again. To help reinforce the fact that the PM should not be used for ongoing support, it's recommended that a different PM be assigned for each new project that relates back to the same product or service. In addition to reducing post-live dependency on a single PM, the PMO will have a more diverse team with more varied work experiences.

Managing Transition Throughout the Plan

The stage is now set for the post-project state with a formal and trained service center, along with strong change management of future requests. Given this infrastructure, we will now explore how PMs can successfully hand off their projects to the operations team. The process for handoff must start as early in the project as possible and continue through project closure. A successful project handoff will feature the following:

1. All roles and responsibilities are defined, understood, and agreed to by project closure.
2. Appropriate documentation is created, accessible, and relevant to the product or service.
3. Any remaining work after the project is complete is identified and assigned to a resource to finalize.
4. Outstanding risks and issues are assigned an owner for ongoing follow-up.
5. Stakeholders and operational staff are well informed of the process for support, and the PM is no longer a point of contact for that product.

Initiating

Although it may seem odd to start the transition process as soon as the project begins, it is critical that customers, stakeholders, and the IT department are in alignment with the long-term expectations for support. One of the major deliverables of project initiating is the development of a project charter. Although the project charter will set the stage for the project itself, including the goals, objectives, and justification, it should also include cost. When we think of the cost of a project, we typically point to the immediate impact on the budget: the cost of the product and the cost of implementation services. While this is important for the scope of the project, the customer, the organization, and the IT department must also understand the total cost of ownership (TCO), including ongoing operation costs. Operation costs should not just include the recurring fees or licenses that are incurred as a result of owning the product, but also the cost of services that may need to extend well beyond the completion of the project, all the way through the disposition of the product. For example, if you had a project to implement a new web-based portal for customers to interact with your organization, you may need to review some of these non-project related costs:

1. A toll-free call center that customers can use for support, staffed with resources that can help route calls to the appropriate group, which may not be IT-related;
2. Marketing staff and materials to ensure that the target customers are aware of the portal and how to access it;
3. Hosting and storage costs, which includes a portion of the data center's operating costs, such as staffing, cooling, power, networking, and physical security;
4. Maintenance costs, including staff time and IT resources to make updates based on new requirements, apply vendor-produced patches and updates, and review and address security vulnerabilities.

Therefore, the organization must be prepared to budget appropriately for ongoing support and maintenance of the new products and services. Likewise, the PM should consider these costs throughout the duration of the project. Often, the PM will make decisions that are aimed at keeping projects in scope, on budget, and on schedule. While those decisions may make the best sense for the short-term life of the project, it's equally important to understand the long-term ramifications of those decisions on the TCO.

A second major component of the initiating process group is the identification of stakeholders. When identifying stakeholders, remember that they include more than just the business partners and team members. A fully defined list of stakeholders should also include end users and the persons or groups that will ultimately support them, such as the service desk, and tier-2 and tier-3 support personnel. Once the stakeholders are identified, this is an excellent opportunity to hold a project transition planning meeting, where all key team members can come to a common understanding that the PM, like the project, is only temporary and has a solitary goal of meeting the project scope on time and within budget. Any existing support infrastructure can be reviewed, and any concerns with the process can be addressed well before handoff begins, while there is still time to implement corrective measures.

Although it may be too early to define all the roles in the project, there is one in particular that needs to be addressed as the project moves into planning: the *product owner*. The owner could be considered the business sponsor, the application administrator, or the product manager. Regardless of what the role is called, there are some key traits that this individual must possess.

1. *Understands the long-term vision of the product*—the owner should have a decisive role in the development of a strategic roadmap for where the product or service will be in the next five years. To that end, the owner should not be a member of the development team, but rather a person in an executive or leadership position in the organization. This will allow them to have a more objective view of new change requests as they are made.

2. *Assumes full ownership of the product*—although the occasional consultation with the PM may be needed in the first couple of weeks or months after the project closure, the owner must understand that the support of the product rests solely on him or her and his or her team. Owners should be in routine contact with the service center and operational staff and serve as an escalation point when issues cannot be resolved at lower levels.

3. *Works closely with staff at all levels in the organization*—understanding that a product should evolve over time to remain relevant, the owner must be the salesperson-in-chief when it comes to their application. There will always be conflicting priorities, particularly in the IT industry, and the owner must continually push for excellence and fast responses to customer requests. Although this may be easier for internally developed solutions, the importance of expediency and efficiency is no less important for applications maintained by external vendors. Recalling our earlier observations that customers will always find the path of least resistance, the owner must be on that path to remain relevant.

4. *Knows when the end is near*—products and services are developed to meet a specific need at a specific point in time. Eventually, new processes and procedures will come into play, and the organization will take different strategic directions. At that point, it's just as important for the product owner to adapt to those changes and find the appropriate time to decommission the old system and replace it with a product that will provide more value to the organization in the future. This is important to keep the project management cycle alive, as well.

At a most basic level, the owner should have the capacity of performing all of the duties the PM had done during the project, except in more of an operational and maintenance role.

Planning

As the project moves into the planning phase, there is an increased opportunity to develop the project team and engage with more resources. During planning, the PM should be certain to perform the following tasks:

1. *Review the project deliverables and determine requirements*—although this is typically part of the project planning process, it's important to make sure requirements are matched to some supporting task by the end of the project. For example, if one of the project deliverables is the deployment of a new server, there should be a process in place to ensure that the server will be maintained after the project is complete. Likewise, requirements should not simply account for the utility of the product (whether it meets appropriate expectations), but also for the warranty of the product (whether it is fit for use). In other words, project requirements must include an assessment of the long-term service module, such as storage requirements, security considerations, continuity of operations, and disaster recovery expectations.

2. *Identify tasks that must be completed by the end of the project versus those that may continue past project closure*—the objectives in the scope of the project are typically the starting point for identifying the project requirements. Knowing these requirements serve two purposes: (1) once all objectives and requirements are met, the project can begin closure and handoff. If there are additional requests that the customer has after viewing the end product, there is a potential that they can be completed through the organization's change management processes (outside of the project), or they could be developed into a new scope for a future project; and (2) there may be some tasks that are deemed important (e.g., the creation of product documentation), but they may not be required for the successful implementation of the project. Knowing what is required and what is optional can help determine some of the roles that may be needed after the project is closed, especially if some of that work will need to continue after the PM steps away.

3. *Define service expectations and measurements for the product/service*—different stakeholders may have different expectations for the management of new products and services. Therefore, there should be an organized and defined plan that measures specific attributes of the system, including:

a. *Downtime definition*—a factor to determine when a service is offline or degraded.

b. *Downtime metrics*—acceptable measurements for total system downtime, such as a 99.99% uptime benchmark.

c. *Scheduled outages*—appropriate times when a production system can be taken offline to perform service, who will be responsible for performing those activities, and specific times when downtime should be avoided, such as during shift changes or other events when usage is expected to be higher than normal.

d. *Response times*—an expected turnaround time for issue resolution based on a rating scale, such as low, medium, high, and critical.

These service expectations can be included in a service level agreement (SLA), which is a commitment between the service provider and the customer. SLAs may also include expectations from the customer, such as certain types of product usage that may not be supported by the service provider. Service expectations would also help to form the foundation of configuration and change management plans. In some cases, a less-formal and non-binding memorandum of understanding (MoU) may be used to express a mutual agreement between the two parties.

4. *Conduct a skill gap analysis for the transition team*—there may be a need for additional training or reviews of existing processes with certain staff. Knowing these requirements up front can allow the PM to incorporate those tasks (and potentially the relevant funding) in the project, well before handoff needs to occur. For example, if you are working on a project to replace outdated technology, such as migrating from an analog telephone system to one that utilizes voice over Internet protocol (VoIP), your existing network and server teams may suddenly need to understand concepts around call management, Federal Communications Commission (FCC) regulations, and quality of service (QoS) metrics. In some cases, this may require an entirely new group of resources that are dedicated to supporting the new technology.

5. *Develop and update a tailored matrix of required roles, resources, and skills*—the foundation to a successful project handoff rests on staff knowing what they are responsible for as early in the process as possible. For example, if you are expecting a tester to perform routine regression testing of an application after the project is complete, they must be involved in the beginning of the project to fully understand how the system works, what needs to be tested, and how that system integrates with any other system in the organization.

Given that the matrix of roles and responsibilities is so crucial to handoff success, take a moment to review the information in Table 13.1 and evaluate how it may align to the products in your own organization. Remember, these are the roles and responsibilities after the project is complete. The project itself may have alternate roles and staffing.

Table 13.1 Transition Roles and Responsibilities

Transition Role	Responsibility
Product/process owner	Primary decision maker for the application and/or process. Works directly with super users and organizational leadership to facilitate the triage of issues and change requests. Responsible for the overall health of the application and/or process. This role is similar to that of the PM and should be defined at the start of the project.
Executive leadership owner	Primary decision maker as it relates to the use of product resources. Works directly with application/process owner on critical issues, change requests, and system downtime. This role is similar to that of the project sponsor. In smaller systems, the executive leadership and product owner may be the same individual.
Super user(s), if needed	Responsible for having a good understanding of the entire front-end product. Acts as an advocate for end-users' needs, ensuring that training and access requirements are met. Escalates issues to the application owner or application admin, as appropriate.
Application administrator	Responsible for the day-to-day maintenance of the overall configuration of the application, including user accounts and security access. Escalates issues to the vendor, as appropriate, and communicates directly with super users or application/process owners.
Database administrator	Responsible for database accessibility, system performance, data replication, and overall system maintenance, including upgrades and patches. Works with all team members when performing maintenance activities under the organization's change management processes.

(Continued)

Table 13.1 *(Continued)*

Transition Role	Responsibility
Server administrator	Responsible for the system hardware and general operating system (OS) and application performance. Allows access to server for applicable individuals and vendor(s). Works with various team members while performing regular server maintenance, such as OS and antivirus updates.
Systems and networking administrator	Responsible for ongoing maintenance of the product's infrastructure, including networking, wireless, and overall system components.
Desktop/user support	Responsible for front-end access to the application or product. Ensures that end-user hardware meets specifications for product, as well as security requirements. Assists administrators during upgrades and other maintenance activities.
Web administrator	Responsible for the administration of any web-based components of a system, including security certifications and renewals.
Product development	Responsible for new configuration and build work in the application (outside of user account maintenance). Works with team members under the organization's change management processes.
Analyst	Responsible for being the primary point of contact with end users during critical issues, such as downtime. For smaller systems, this role can be merged with other roles in the support team.
Testing lead	Responsible for ongoing testing of any aspect of the application, product, or process. Ensures testing coverage during maintenance activities.
Training lead	Responsible for ensuring that all staff is trained before access to the system is granted. Works with the application administrator to manage user account and security access as users are added or removed from the system.
Help desk	Responsible for tier-1 support of the application or process. Works with all team members to ensure that issues and tickets are routed, assigned, and communicated appropriately.
General operations	Responsible for off-hours support and regular monitoring of the system, as appropriate.

Execution

By the time the project is underway with assigned staff and resources, the elements that were determined during planning should be reflected throughout the project. The PM should work with project stakeholders to assign individuals to the roles and responsibilities matrix that was created during project planning. Involving the support team in the project this early can be challenging, as these individuals likely have other operational (and even other project) responsibilities, and they may take the stance of, "just let me know what you need when the project is finished." However, the PM must insist that these individuals are represented throughout the project. Although they may not need to attend every meeting, they should at least be kept informed of the project's progress through meeting minutes, status reports, and other ongoing documentation. Additionally, early involvement can help prompt the need for documentation, training, and security access that may otherwise be missed. If the PM makes the mistake of waiting until the end of the project to start this transition, it will be doomed to failure, leaving the PM as the sole bearer of full knowledge of the product's history.

As the project nears completion, the PM should conduct a readiness assessment for the organization's operations team. The assessment should determine if the service desk knows what the product/service is, where issues should be reported, and how tickets should be routed. In the days and weeks leading up to go-live, the PM should be having multiple conversations with the organization's support team(s) and their leadership to answer questions and provide details. An increase in trouble calls can be expected in the first few weeks of a product release, and you certainly do not want confused end users to encounter even more confused support staff. Keep in mind that unless there is a dedicated support center for this specific product, tier-1 agents will be responsible for fielding queries from multiple sources, addressing a range of products and services. Thus, it is equally important that there are reference documents readily available that describe how to handle trouble calls, often referred to as knowledge base articles (KBAs) or job aids. The reference documents should provide simple, clear instructions to the customer service agent and may include background information about the product, workflow diagrams, answers to frequently asked questions, and details about how to route calls or service tickets, should additional tiers of support be needed.

Additionally, the PM should be working to finalize any necessary SLAs between the customer and operations team. Optimally, there should be a process in place to ensure compliance with the SLA, which can be accomplished through ticketing systems, reporting services, and assessments and surveys. Both the customer and provider should also have a common understanding as to where this product falls in priority with respect to other services provided by the operations team. In the event of a failure of multiple systems, which may occur during data center or network problems, there should be a prioritization list, which clearly defines the order of restoration across the organization's portfolio. The priority should be correlated to the mission of the organization and based on the potential impact if the system is unavailable. This is often documented in a document called a business impact assessment (BIA).

This is also an opportune time to create or revise any standard operating procedures (SOPs), which provide a straightforward step-by-step guide for completing certain tasks against the product that is going live. SOPs help to ensure consistency and accountability when handing production-level activities, while decreasing the potential for errors. These procedures should be developed with the resources that will be providing support, and they should be reviewed and tested prior to production activities to validate their accuracy.

Finally, every effort should be made to help limit the calls that will come into the support center. Providing staff with user guides is a good start, but they are often lengthy and go unread by busy staff. Instead, provide quick reference guides in the forms of leaflets, postcards, and signage. The PM should ensure that the assignment and completion of post-live project documentation is included in the project work plan and communicated to the project team well enough in advance so they can be completed on time. It is possible that some complex and noncritical documentation could be completed after the project is closed.

Table 13.2 provides a list of deliverables that can play a critical role to the success of the product or service after the project is complete. Note that this may be tailored from project to project, based on the complexity of the product, the skill set of the operations team, and the support expectations of the customer.

Closing

By the end of the project, the PM should be fully prepared for a successful handoff to support. It is common for the PM to remain involved with the day-to-day support for a fixed timeframe after the product has gone

Table 13.2   Post-live Project Documentation

Deliverable	Description	Author
Administrator guide	Typically provided by the vendor or builder of the product, describes the configuration and features available for application administrators.	Vendor, application administrator
User guide	Typically provided by the vendor or builder of the product, provides a "how to" guide for the end user.	Vendor, application administrator
Configuration management plan	Describes how post-project change requests will be submitted, triaged, and implemented.	Change management team
Troubleshooting tips/checklist/ guidelines	Provides an overview of common issues and questions that could be encountered when using the product or service; this document should be regularly updated based on customer feedback.	Super user, process owner
Knowledge base articles (KBAs)	Describes the process for triaging, tracking, and assigning issues that transpire after the project is completed.	PM, application administrator
How-to quick reference guide	Provides a summarized version of the user guide for common questions or frequently used features; this should be as simple as possible, such as a postcard or single-page leaflet.	Super user
Service level agreement (SLA)	Describes an agreement between two parties, such as the customer and operations, or the customer and the vendor; there are legal implications for not adhering to set guidelines around support and maintenance.	PM, executive owner, process owner
Business impact assessment (BIA)	Establishes business continuity requirements by aligning a product to the mission of the organization and the impact of a disruption of its service	Process owner, application administrator, executive owner

(Continued)

Table 13.2 *(Continued)*

Deliverable	Description	Author
Memorandum of understanding (MoU)	Describes an agreement between two parties, such as the customer and operations, or the customer and the vendor; there is no legal or binding power, but rather a mutual understanding.	Vendor, executive owner, process owner
Standard operating procedure (SOP)	Provides step-by-step instructions on performing certain administrative or operational tasks against the application to ensure consistency.	Application admin, server admin, database admin
Project summary and reference document	Describes the project that was implemented and where to locate additional product details for future reference.	PM

live. However, the period of time for the PM to be involved should optimally be limited to two weeks, or up to four weeks for major, complex implementations. It is critical that the customer and the PM understand and agree to this timeframe so the project can be closed. During this time, the PM should review all of the post-live documentation that was created, and keep it updated with known errors and workarounds. To ensure that your support staff have the information needed to do their job well, it may be necessary to provide an in-service training to help communicate project information and to answer any questions about the documentation provided. You may even want to assign project team members to sit with support staff in the first week or two after activation, just to validate the post-live processes and procedures are working as intended. Copies of the documentation may also be provided to the customer to reassure them that they will be in good hands. It may also be beneficial for the PM to include the customer in any lessons learned discussions, so that feedback can also be incorporated into the support documentation.

Any remaining tasks or issues should be assigned an owner for post-live follow-up, and those assignments should be made available to the customer for reference purposes. Once the business owner has been notified of the production support procedures and the project sponsor has accepted completion of the project, the project can be closed and ownership duties can officially be transferred from the PM.

Case Study 1: Implementation of an Electronic Health Record

Type: Commercial-off-the-shelf (COTS)

Additional Information

An organization has decided to replace their electronic health record (EHR). This EHR is a COTS product, provided by a large and well-known vendor, and it will replace a solution that had been used in the hospital for the past decade. The new EHR promises to include a host of new features that were lacking in the original system, such as integration with other hospital systems, new reporting capabilities, and access through mobile devices. Although the hospital has always had its own dedicated IT department, most of the staff has had to acquire new skills, and teams that typically did not have a significant role with the EHR, such as network staff and device management staff, have suddenly become integral to the operations and support of the system. Since the EHR is supplied by an external vendor, there will still be some reliance on the vendor to troubleshoot issues that are beyond the capacity of the internal IT team.

Questions

1. What roles would need to be included in the transition to support?
2. What types of documentation would need to be created?
3. How long should the PM remain involved with the project, post-live?

Feedback

Feedback for this case study can be found in Appendix A.

Case Study 2: Implementation of an Organizational Metrics Dashboard

Type: Custom development

Additional Information

The PM assigned to the implementation of the metrics dashboard gained a favorable reputation with her customers and colleagues. She has been with the organization for several years and knows who to go to in order to resolve issues. She has the ability to find creative solutions to complex problems and does everything she can to keep things running smoothly, on-time, and on-budget. Being the exceptional PM that she is, she started planning for the transition of the dashboard to the IT department staff early in the project. She ensured that knowledge articles, SOPs, and other reference guides were created and distributed to support staff, whom she refers to as her partners in the project. Since everything was managed so well, the number of issues after go-live was minimal, and the project was closed. Almost a year later, the support center received a call reporting that an executive was unable to access the dashboard to create a monthly report. While the agent tried to help, he was only on the job for a few months and was not familiar with the system and misrouted the ticket. Several hours passed without a response, so the frustrated executive called the PM directly, pleading for help.

Questions

1. How should the PM respond to the customer?
2. Who is responsible for training new support staff on existing systems?

Feedback

Feedback for this case study can be found in Appendix A.

Chapter 14

Measuring Success

Patricia P. Sengstack

> The question for the future is not "What do you do?" or "How do you do it?" but rather, "What difference have you made?"

American Nurses Credentialing Center, 2010

Measuring the success or outcome of a project can be viewed from two perspectives, both of which require attention at the time of project initiation. First, the evaluation of the implementation itself is essential to project managers, as the information obtained can be used as lessons learned for future projects. This perspective of the evaluation process includes determining whether or not the project met major milestones on time, whether there were budget overruns, whether key deliverables were implemented, whether resource allocation was appropriate, and whether the final system met all defined requirements.

The second perspective of the evaluation process addresses whether or not the project met the overall business need and the reason the project was funded and supported by the organization. This chapter will briefly review the first perspective but will focus on the second perspective of the evaluation process.

Project success has traditionally been measured as being completed on time and on budget. While these are wonderful goals, they offer a narrow viewpoint and do not address whether the final deliverables matched the requirements, were acceptable by the customer, or even met the desired need.

Success factors around time and cost measure the project management methodology, but not necessarily all the activities of the project or if the

DOI: 10.4324/9781003206668-14

need was met. It is critical that the criteria of success be defined early in the project, as the project is being defined. Project sponsors or key stakeholders are often the people who define these criteria.

Project success factors can be derived from the documents developed during the initiation and planning phase. Measuring whether the final software delivered matches the requirements that were approved at the beginning of the project, plus any approved changes, would be one example. Another is if the plan includes migrating data from a legacy system, was it migrated successfully and in the expected format? Success factors also can come from any project constraints or assumptions. An example would be successfully utilizing the current hardware based on the assumption that no new hardware would be required. The project success factors should be measured by the time the project ends.

Earned value management (EVM) is a project management tool to measure project performance throughout the project. These calculations help to track the performance over time comparing actual performance against the baseline or planned performance. A table with some of the more common EVM calculations is included in the Appendix B.

TIP

The identified evaluation methodology should measure the quality and effectiveness of any software implementation.

Each information technology (IT) investment is undertaken for a reason. With significant financial investments in software, it is important to develop and implement a strategy to assess and confirm that the expected benefits are realized. Most of these evaluation activities will be completed after the project's go-live.

Did the new computerized provider order entry (CPOE) system reduce medication errors? Did the new admission, discharge, and transfer system result in fewer duplicate patient records? Did the new electronic nursing documentation module result in more accurate clinical data? Did it reduce the amount of time nurses spend charting? Did the new system really make a difference?

This perspective of system evaluation looks at the organization's strategic objectives for undertaking the project. Some of these objectives might not be realized until months after the project officially ends, but a comprehensive evaluation is essential to ensure that the organization's time and money, both of which are significant, are well spent.

Clinical information systems are a major investment for healthcare organizations, not just in terms of dollars, but also in human resources. This significant expenditure for implementing, upgrading, and enhancing these systems requires evaluation and justification.

It should be common sense that resources should go toward the implementation of safe and effective systems, but measuring this becomes difficult or is often ignored. With clear justification, organizations are beginning to demand outcome data from their investments in IT. The measurement of a system's success or effectiveness needs to be given consideration at the time of project planning.

Measuring outcomes from a system implementation is as variable as the projects themselves. The evaluation of each project is unique and based on multiple factors, including the organizational need, the desired outcome, and the data and resources available to perform the evaluation work.

A project's outcome may be measured in a number of areas:

- Clinical outcomes
- Reduction in episodes of ventilator-acquired pneumonia with the implementation of electronic order sets and/or appropriate reminders and alerts
- Increased compliance with vaccinations or other routine examinations
- Financial outcomes
- Reduction in or elimination of paper/toner
- Reduction in duplicate processes/systems by centralization of systems
- Research outcomes
- Improved accuracy of data to support research
- Improved access to data by researchers
- System adoption
- Increased use of system or component by physicians
- Increased use of system or component by nurses and other care providers
- User satisfaction
- End-user satisfaction level with new system
- Usability of system is satisfactory
- Quality/patient safety

- Reduction in medication errors
- Improved accuracy of data for clinical decision-making
- Administrative outcomes
- Improved administrative report accuracy
- Improved access to administrative data
- Productivity
- Reduction in time to document in new system
- Workflow process streamlined

From these examples, it becomes clear that a one-size-fits-all evaluation process to measure the outcome of an implementation project does not exist. It must be customized to fit the specific desired need and expected outcomes. The plan can be derived from the documents developed in the initiation and planning phases.

It is at this point in the project that the organization's overall objective or outcome should be clarified. Oftentimes, the evaluation will require that baseline data be collected so that a comparison can be made at designated time intervals post go-live. This emphasizes the importance of investing time during the project's planning phase to think about and document how a project will be evaluated once the system is activated.

The project manager may not be involved in these measurements, as they are often conducted months or even years after the project ends. However, they should provide input into the process during the project and include any qualifiers that may impact the data collected pre- or post-activation.

For example, medication errors may appear to increase after the implementation of CPOE, and leadership might attribute this to a failed implementation. However, studies indicate that electronically collected data are more accurate than manually collected data; error rates are not actually higher with CPOE, just more accurate. Tracking trends over a period of time after CPOE go-live will provide a better indication of the success of the implementation.

Determining what to measure can be a challenge. While quantitative data are typically preferred, the need for qualitative data is clear in the areas of user satisfaction and user experience with the new system. Along with the increased importance of evaluating outcomes, literature and industry tools for evaluation have appeared.

The Agency for Healthcare Research and Quality's (AHRQ's) Health Information Technology Evaluation Toolkit (2009) is a valuable tool for determining what data to collect based on the project and desired outcome being measured.

In addition, the National Resource Center developed a compendium of health IT surveys that may meet the needs of a particular project's evaluation. Both the surveys and toolkit are available on AHRQ's web site.

A thorough outcomes evaluation also should include a core set of standard components in areas such as the methodology, results, discussion, and conclusion.

There are a number of resources available to provide guidance and best practices for developing an evaluation plan to measure outcomes related to quality, rigor, and applicability to the development of a customized plan. Other resources include several organizations that focus on healthcare quality; some are listed at the end of this chapter.

TIP

For each project, an organization should measure the success of the project itself and the success of meeting the need for which the project is intended.

Key to the success of an outcomes evaluation plan is the involvement of the business owners and senior stakeholders. Also, consider the involvement of the organization's central quality council, if one exists. These stakeholders are most familiar with the business need for the new system and can provide valuable input as the outcome objectives and the evaluation plan are developed. The outcomes evaluation plan should include the following:

- Expected outcomes or objectives
- Operational definitions of each outcome
- Points at which objectives are measured
- Resources needed
- Role of each resource defined
- Determination of the need for baseline data
- Data collection plan

These details are defined in the plan, which should be approved by the project sponsors and are a key deliverable for the project. Any activities identified in the plan that occur during the project should be included in the project schedule. Once the project is complete, the work should continue according to the schedule in the strategic metrics plan.

When new software and workflow processes are introduced, there is a period of adjustment while the users are learning and understanding the changes. Any measurements taken during this time will be influenced by the learning curve, which will skew the outcomes. Depending on the size of the change, this may continue 3, 6, or even 12 months after activation. Data evaluation should take this into account, and the farther out from the activation, the more accurate the steady state should be.

Evaluating the system implementation should reflect the breadth of potential outcomes that can result. So many questions can be asked and evaluated. What are the attitudes of users toward the software or even the new processes that came with the software? How well are they adapting to the new technology? What are patients' perceptions of the new processes? Do care providers spend the entire time with the patient looking at the computer? Do the patients perceive this as a distraction? What are the financial impacts of the new software? How long will it take to recover the cost of the implementation?

Simply measuring these outcomes is not enough; the data should be measured and decisions should be made based on the results. The goal is to continuously improve the quality, safety, and user satisfaction, as well as to reduce costs. The key is to allocate the time and resources to evaluate the outcome of system implementation, starting in the planning phase.

Some organizations that focus on healthcare quality and safety include the following:

- The Joint Commission (www.jointcommission.org)
- The Agency for Healthcare Research and Quality (AHRQ) (www.ahrq.gov)
- The National Quality Forum (www.qualityforum.org)
- Institute for Healthcare Improvement (www.ihi.org)
- National Association for Healthcare Quality (www.nahq.org)
- American Health Quality Association (www.ahqa.org)
- Leapfrog Group (www.leapfroggroup.org)
- National Committee for Quality Assurance (www.ncqa.org)

Case Study 1: Implementation of an Electronic Health Record

Type: Commercial off-the-shelf

Additional Information

Your activation was successful and the end users are working through the expected workflow issues and trying to remember how to use the system. You have staff providing at-the-elbow assistance to end users to support them during the transition.

Questions

1. What metrics would you use to measure the success of the project implementation itself?
2. What metrics would you use to measure the success of meeting the strategic objectives?

Feedback

Feedback for this case study can be found in Appendix A.

Case Study 2: Implementation of an Organizational Metrics Dashboard

Type: Custom development

Additional Information

Your activation was successful, and metrics data is starting to be collected and displayed in the new metrics dashboard. Some metrics are not scheduled to be collected for a few months. You had staff providing support during the go-live of the dashboard, and it was appreciated. You have also provided a user's manual for those who might not use the system right away.

Questions

1. What metrics would you use to measure the success of the metrics dashboard project itself?
2. What metrics would you use to measure the success of meeting the strategic objectives?

Feedback

Feedback for this case study can be found in Appendix A.

Appendix A
Case Study Feedback

Discussions for Case Studies

This section provides feedback for the case study questions presented at the end of the chapters. You were only provided with minimal information about the case studies prior to being asked the questions. If you were actually managing these projects/programs, however, you would have considerably more information at hand to make decisions. Further, it is important to note that some decisions are based on the culture of the organization rather than best practices. Also, please remember there are no right or wrong answers.

Chapter 2: Project, Program, and Portfolio Management

Case Study 1: Implementation of an Electronic Health Record

Type: Commercial off-the-shelf (COTS)

Included Functionality

- Prescription drug monitoring program (PDMP) for opioid management
- Research protocol order sets, and advanced clinical documentation
- Provide advanced clinical documentation for patient care staff

Current Situation

Your organization has an electronic health record (EHR) system from a well-known vendor. You have been assigned to implement the additional functionality listed above, which is now available. Upon review of your current situation, you learn that the functionality is only available with the latest version of the system, therefore an upgrade will also be required.

Questions

1. Would this implementation be managed as a project or a program?

   While this could be managed as a project, it would be best managed as a program. This implementation has the possibility of being very large and would benefit from being broken down into separate projects, with someone managing the day-to-day work for each. This would also benefit from having separate stakeholder groups who can focus on working with the project teams. If managed as a single project, it would still be beneficial to have separate workgroups for each.

2. If managed as a program, how would you break it up into separate related projects?

   There are a variety of ways to separate this program into individual related projects. The following is a list of potential projects:
   – PDMP for opioid management
   – Research protocol order sets
     • This could even be broken down further based on specific criteria, such as physician group, department (intensive care, emergency department, etc.), or by specialty (oncology, cardiology, etc.)
   – Research clinical documentation:
     • This could also be broken down further into the same criteria as above.
       ▪ Advanced clinical documentation for patient care staff

Case Study 2: Implementation of a Research Tracking System

Type: Custom development

Included Functionality

- Allow online data entry as well as upload from spreadsheets
- Provide a method for the end users to query and report on the data
- Provide ability to ensure users only have access to their research data

Current Situation

You have been asked to develop software to help manage multiple research studies. This will replace the multiple spreadsheets currently in use to track the data. Upon review of the current situation, you find that there are multiple studies in progress and the researchers want to limit who has access to their data. The request for reports includes the ability for the user to query the data through a user-friendly tool and produce reports ad hoc based on the queries.

Questions

1. Would this implementation be managed as a project or a program?

    This is appropriate to be managed as a single project.

2. If managed as a program, how would you break it up into separate related projects?

    Not applicable due to the option chosen.

Chapter 3: Project Process Groups

Case Study 1: Implementation of an Electronic Health Record

Type: COTS

Additional Information

The vendor offers a full suite of functionality and modules for the hospital, which includes an emergency department (ED) module. Currently, the ED does order entry in the main hospital system, but the clinical documentation is still on paper.

Questions

1. What types of training might be included in the training plan for this project/program?

   – Introduction: provides basic navigation processes, for example, how to find the clinical documentation from the ED visit. This would be beneficial for all users, including those with view-only access.
   – Clinical documentation: provides education on how to document through the different methods available, such as flowsheets, structured notes, free-text notes, and even the eMAR for medications. This would be useful for anyone documenting on an ED patient.

2. What might be some challenges faced by the project/program team?

   One of the largest challenges would be around coordination and communication. Due to the variability of patient flow in an ED, it will be difficult scheduling meetings with staff unless additional coverage is made available or they are done off-shift. Both options can be costly in staff pay.

3. What roles, or skill sets, would be required for the project/program team?

   The following is a list of roles that might be required for this program. Depending on the work effort required, and how much time the staff has to dedicate to the program, multiple people may be needed within each role.
   – Program sponsor(s)
   – Program manager(s)
   – Application administrators/configuration
   – Business analysts/workflow analysis
   – Report developer
   – Interface developer
   – Testers
   – Trainers
   – Help desk/support staff

Case Study 2: Implementation of a Research Tracking System

Type: Custom development

Additional Information

There are a limited number of people, approximately 15, who will initially use the new tracking system to manage four different research protocols. It has been identified that other teams are also interested in using the system for their research. One goal identified early is for the new system to be web-based for easy access.

Questions

1. What types of training might be included in the training plan for this project/program?

   With the limited number of users for this new system, training might include a demo to all, along with a user manual for reference. Another option would be to have super users to provide one-on-one training to the users regarding how to enter their research data. The latter might be a better option if the different teams have different workflows within the new system.

2. What might be some challenges faced by the project/program team?

   The challenges for this project are related to obtaining good requirements and controlling the scope. When the owners cannot see something to say they like, don't like, or cannot see specific functionality, it is hard to gather all requirements. They often do not verbalize everything they have in their minds as to expected functionality or the way they want the system to look and feel. This is the reason why more development models include a prototype or follow an iterative process. The challenge is to control how many iteration steps will be completed prior to it being "done" or at least how many prior to bringing the other teams on board.

3. What roles, or skill sets, would be required for the project/program team?

   The following is a list of roles that might be required for this project. Depending on the work effort required, and how much time the staff has to dedicate to the project, multiple people might be needed within each role. Also, on some projects, one person might be able to fill multiple roles. For example, the application developer might also serve as the report developer; the business analyst might also serve as the tester or trainer. This would depend on their skill set and availability.

– Project sponsor(s)
– Project manager(s)
– Business analyst/requirements
– Application developer
– Report developer
– Systems administrator
– Database administrator
– Testers
– Trainers
– Help desk/support staff

Chapter 4: Project Knowledge Areas

Case Study 1: Implementation of an Electronic Health Record

Type: COTS

Additional Information

The vendor provides a standard WBS work plan that outlines a 16-month implementation plan. The new hardware has been ordered. They have assigned the following resources:

■ Project manager: to manage vendor work and resources
■ Trainer: to provide training for project team and super users
■ Clinical consultant: to facilitate workflow redesign
■ Configuration consultant: to provide guidance and assistance for system build and customization
■ Technical specialist: to provide guidance and assistance for the technical configuration related to hardware and database
■ Technical interface specialist: to provide guidance and assistance for the interface development

Questions

1. What types of requirements are needed for this project/program?

   The contracting documentation should have a list of all requirements the organization was looking for related to what they purchased. For the program tasks, there are a number of requirements that need to be defined and approved. The vendor is providing a system with a lot of functionality, but your organization might not choose to implement all of it due to their implementation strategy or because they do not offer the service that fits with the features. During the project-planning phase, a decision should be made regarding what functionality will be implemented and what will not. This should be part of the scope document and should be managed as part of the scope. Additional requirements would include the following:
   - Reports: this includes what reports the users will view, or print, what information will be included, and how will they look. It is wise to include the medical records department if any reports will become part of the permanent medical record.
   - Interfaces: this includes the requirements regarding what information is to be included in each interface, the flow of the data, what manipulation is necessary and where will it be done, and the location of each data element within the Health Level 7 (HL7) message.
   - Clinical documentation: this includes what terminology will be used and exactly what will be built. The importance of gaining consensus across the entire organization on how the documentation will be done cannot be understated. With that said, this should be fully documented and approved before any configuration is completed.
   Changes to all requirements should be controlled through a change management process similar to the scope management process.

   What types of line items would you expect to find on the budget? The budget for this program could include the following:
   - Software licenses from vendor
   - Software licenses for any third-party applications necessary for vendor's software to function (i.e., database licenses)
   - Hardware, including servers and workstations
   - Professional services from vendor for their staff to assist with implementation
   - Contract staff, if your organization requires supplemental staffing for this program

- Training for the project team, which might be offered onsite, online, or at the vendor's location

2. Who would you expect to be stakeholders for this project/program?

   The stakeholders would include the entire program team, all physicians, all nurses, all other users of the system, medical records; radiology; and laboratory departments, admissions, and the organization's leadership.

3. What methods of communication might the project manager utilize for this project/program?

   The project manager could use any number of the following methods of communication. This is not an exhaustive list, so be creative when communicating on any project or program.
   - Meeting minutes
   - Town hall meetings
   - Steering or governance committees
   - Department staff meetings
   - Flyers
   - E-mails
   - Newsletters
   - Booth/table near cafeteria
   - Web-sites

Case Study 2: Implementation of an Organizational Metrics Dashboard

Type: Custom development

Additional Information

The project sponsor has identified key people with whom the team should work to define requirements. They will be the super users who can also assist with testing. An experienced developer from the IT department will develop the new system. He will develop the software using a development platform/technology he has used in the past and it can be hosted on current servers in the data center.

Questions

1. What types of requirements are needed for this project/program?

   This project should include business requirements that define each metric, the data collected, including the format, and the details around what is expected for dashboard view. The design requirements might be separate or may be combined with the business requirements. Any requested reports also should be defined in the requirements.

2. What types of line items would you expect to find on the budget?

   The budget for this program could include the following items:
   - Software licenses for platform used for development
   - Software licenses for any third-party applications necessary for software to function (i.e., database licenses)
   - Hardware, including servers, if necessary
   - Contract staff, if your organization requires supplemental staffing for this project

3. Who would you expect to be stakeholders for this project/program?

   The stakeholders for this project include the project team, the staff who collect the metrics, the organization leadership who will view the dashboard, and anyone else involved in the workflow or data flow.

4. What methods of communication might the project manager utilize for this project/program?

   The project manager could use any number of the following methods of communication. This is not an exhaustive list, so please be creative when communicating on any project.
   - Meeting minutes
   - E-mails
   - Stakeholder meetings
   - Websites

Chapter 5: Software Development Lifecycle

Case Study 1: Implementation of an Electronic Health Record

Type: COTS

Additional Information

The vendor has provided details about how the new system can be customized. The organization can decide and build the following:

- Order sets that can be used for Opioid medications or research protocols
- Alerts based on recent Opioid orders for the patient
- Format used for clinical documentation
- How clinical documentation is displayed once entered
- Reports to be displayed and printed from the system

Question

1. What phases would this project/program include?

    This program would probably include the following phases, which are more general. Depending on the decision about how to break the program into projects, some projects might not include all of these phases.
    - Program initiation
    - Program planning
    - Workflow analysis and redesign (may be part of planning)
    - Requirements definition (may be part of planning)
    - Program/project team training
    - Application configuration (to include reports)
    - Interface development for pharmacy
    - System testing
    - End-user training
    - Activation
    - Post-live support

Case Study 2: Implementation of an Organizational Metrics Dashboard

Type: Custom development

Additional Information

The following functionality is being requested:

- Allow direct data entry for four independent research studies
- Provide the ability to load the past two years' worth of data
- Provide dashboard views of data with the ability to click on any value to view more details

Question

1. What phases would this project/program include?

   This project would probably include the following phases, which are more general. Depending on the development strategy decision some projects might not include all of these phases. If following an iterative development model, the development would be completed through multiple iterative cycles and testing, training, and activation would follow a release cycle.
   - Project initiation
   - Project planning
   - Requirements definition (may be part of planning)
   - Application development following the development strategy
   - System testing
   - End-user training
   - Activation
   - Post-live support

Chapter 6: Agile Development Methodology

No case study is provided from Chapter 6.

Chapter 7: Choosing the Right Methodology

Case Study 1: Implementation of an Electronic Health Record

Type: COTS

Additional Information

Given that this is COTS software that will impact many employees, you are trying to decide which project management methodology makes sense. As a newly minted project manager, you that see that business users understand their requirements and there is some urgency around moving from paper-based documentation to the new EHR functionality; however, they are generally too busy caring for patients to provide frequent feedback during the project. In addition, the organization has a central PMO. As the project manager, you are required to provide specific project documentation (e.g., project charter, a detailed work breakdown and schedule, requirements and design documents, etc.) and gain approval via Stage Gates reviews for each phase to continue to the next phase. Finally, it's important that the system be fully functional and there is minimal downtime because if it is not near perfect at go-live, it could impact the quality of patient care.

Questions

1. What are some significant project variables that might impact your choice of a project management methodology?

    If the organization wanted a custom developed application and they did not know what the final product should look like, then Agile might be a better approach. However, the first clue in this scenario is that the organization has opted to integrate an off-the-shelf product (that has already been developed based on known requirements), rather than developing their own custom application. The need for quality and minimal downtime—over speed—is also relevant as is the need for documentation and following a formal Stage Gate process. The culture of the organization is based on safety first for the patients and is likely to be risk averse. The stakeholders are too busy to participate much in the project and frequent product owner feedback is needed for Agile to be effective. All these factors suggest that Waterfall methodology may be the best choice for this project.

2. Is there a case for using a hybrid methodology and if so, how would you implement it?

    The Waterfall approach means that there will likely be a freeze on improvements to the existing system, and a "big bang" type of deployment. There is time pressure to get the new system into full production as quickly as possible. The go-live will need to be as perfect as possible; making users wait for a full cut-over at go-live could be a risky choice. A risk mitigation strategy might be to bring in some aspects of the Agile methodology into the effort. The project team could do this by having both the legacy and new systems run in parallel and incrementally migrating capabilities from the old to the new. This method comes with increased technical costs (e.g., you may need an interface between the two systems during the transition), but it allows the development team to gradually release discrete functionality into production in the new system with the ability to roll-back to the old system if necessary. In addition, the development team could incorporate Kanban boards, daily meetings, regular sprint backlog retrospectives and reviews with the users, etc. into their process.

Case Study 2: Implementation of an Organizational Metrics Dashboard

Type: Custom development

Additional Information

A small team made up of members from the matrixed organization has been assigned to build this new custom metrics dashboard. Executives are not exactly sure what they want, but they'll know it when they see it. There is pressure to "do something" and to produce innovative results quickly. The new CEO has asked for organizational performance metrics and is expecting modern analytics. Executive assistants (who will actually use the system to generate reports) have agreed to spend 25% of their time acting as product owners. You got certified as a Scrum Master recently and several of the developers have been involved in Scrum projects before, so you feel confident that the development team could handle an Agile project. The methodology has been used a few times, but it is still relatively new to the organization.

Questions

1. What are some significant project variables that might impact your choice of a project management methodology?

   Two the key features about this scenario are that the stakeholders are unsure at the onset about what needs to be built and that they need you to "do something" quickly. Although the executives who might use the data cannot participate, their assistants can, and they are the main users of the system. Assuming the executive assistants know what their bosses want, at least there will be an avenue for continuous feedback since they have agreed to commit time to it. The organization is somewhat new to Agile, but you and your small group of developers both have a degree of knowledge and experience using Scrum. In this case, your team could use Agile principles to develop a working application relatively quickly and then improve upon that foundation with short sprints based on feedback. Note that it may require the Scrum Master to educate and gain commitment from the other stakeholders to participate in the Agile process.

2. How will you handle stakeholders that don't understand the Agile development processes?

An effective Scrum Master not only knows "what to do" but can also explain the "how" and "why" to all stakeholders involved. Agile is fairly new to this organization, you will likely face resistance and may need to advocate for using this methodology. Yet, you still need to establish an environment where the team can be successful. Stakeholders will need to know their respective roles and have a solid understanding of Scrum procedures. For this project, you will rely heavily on your interpersonal skills to effectively teach, negotiate, facilitate, resolve differences, and mentor stakeholders. During sprints, backlog grooming and retrospectives, the Scrum Master will need to coach the team and stakeholders to adhere to Scrum practices and rules. The Scrum master, rather than the Project Manager, will also host regular meetings to share updates and liaise with product owners about how the project is progressing (or not). These interactions offer opportunities to strengthen the relationship between the team and product owner as well as others outside the team. A large part of the job for the Scrum master, especially in this case, will be to help everyone to understand and follow the process.

Chapter 8: Stakeholder Management

Case Study 1: Implementation of an Electronic Health Record

Type: COTS

Additional Information

The project includes the emergency department (ED) and will include new workflows for clinical documentation by the nurses.

Questions

1. Who are the stakeholders?

   The stakeholders are dependent on who will be entering and using the clinical documentation entered by the ED nurses. If the patient is admitted, the inpatient staff would have access. If the patient is discharged, the ambulatory clinical staff may have access depending on if there is integration with the system used in the ambulatory setting. The patients could have access depending on the data included in the discharge summary and the patient portal, if in place. The information technology department who are implementing this functionality are also stakeholders, including those who are part of the project team and those who will provide support after the project. With these in mind, the stakeholders could include the following:
   - Nurses in the ED (primary end users)
   - All staff in the ED
   - Inpatient staff
   - Ambulatory staff
   - Patients
   - Project team
   - IT help desk staff

2. What types of communication should be included in the project?

   The PM would use the stakeholder analysis as an input to build the communications plan and decide what each member will need to do their work during and after the project's go-live. On example is the ED nurses will need to know how to enter their documentation. Other clinical staff may only need to know how to find and view the documentation. The project team will need a different level of details surrounding the changes being made to the system. With these considerations, the types of communication could include any of the following.
   - Requirements
   - Activation details (dates, times, tasks, durations, etc.)

- System configuration, or build, details
- Lessons learned from throughout the project
- Training details
- System design documentation
- Frequently asked questions (FAQs)
- Support call and troubleshooting guides

3. What is the best method of communication for each?

When determining the communication method, it is important to understand how each stakeholder receives information. For example, the ED nurses do not have time to check email throughout their shifts so this may not be the best way, or should not be the only way, communication to them occurs. The stakeholder analysis will help to identify the expectations each has for the method, frequency, and level of detail for communications. For most end users, multiple methods are usually best to ensure the message is received. Below are options for the methods of communication for this scenario.

- Technical documentation
- Meeting minutes
- Email
- Training, which may include instructor led classes, practice exercises, or computer-based training (CBT)
- Quick reference "how-to" guides
- Flyers
- Bulletins
- Attending user meetings such as shift change or staff meetings
- Status reports
- Updated knowledge base articles for support staff

Case Study 2: Implementation of a Research Tracking System

Type: Custom development

Additional Information

The new research tracking system includes users from four different protocols. It has been requested to keep the workflows the same for all protocols, current and future. This will improve the ability to extend the use in the future without needing to customize for each group.

Questions

1. Who are the stakeholders?

   The stakeholders are dependent on who will be entering and using the research data. The research staff will be following the defined workflows for data entry, analysis, and creation of reports. The additional stakeholders will include anyone who will receive information from the system, either the analysis output or actual reports. These could be internal committees, such as a review board, or external, such as a pharmaceutical partner. The information technology department who are implementing this functionality are also stakeholders, including those who are part of the project team and those who will provide support after the project. With these in mind, the stakeholders could include the following:
   - Research staff (primary end user)
   - Organizational leadership (reviewing reports)
   - Internal Review Board (IRB)
   - External research entities such as a regulatory or partner organizations
   - IT department—development project team

2. What types of communication should be included in the project?

   The PM would use the stakeholder analysis as an input to build the communications plan. This will determine what information each will need to do their work during and after the project's go-live. On example is the research staff will need to know how to enter data, run reports, or access any analysis tools. The consumers of the reports will need to be aware of what data is included, and how it is laid out in the report. They may also be involved in determining the requirements for their specific reports. The project team will need a different level of details surrounding the requirements to be developed into system. With these considerations, the types of communication could include any of the following:
   - Requirements
   - System design

- Technical architecture
- Activation details (dates, times, tasks, durations, etc.)
- Lessons learned from throughout the project
- Training details
- System design documentation
- Frequently asked questions (FAQs)
- Support call and troubleshooting guides

3. What is the best method of communication for each?

When determining the communication method, it is important to understand how each stakeholder receives information. For example, the research staff who do data entry may be at their computers most of the day and can monitor emails, the principle researchers' daily workload may not allow them access to email as easily. The stakeholder analysis will help to identify the expectations each has for the method, frequency, and level of detail for communications. For most end users, multiple methods are usually best to ensure the message is received. Below are options for the methods of communication for this scenario.

- Requirements, design, and technical documentation
- Meeting minutes
- Email
- Training, which may include instructor led classes, practice exercises, or computer-based training (CBT)
- Quick reference "how-to" guides
- Flyers
- Bulletins
- Attending user meetings such as the IRB or research meetings
- Status reports
- Updated knowledge base articles for support staff
- Sample reports once developed

Chapter 9: System Configuration

Case Study 1: Implementation of an Electronic Health Record

Type: COTS

Additional Information

Your analysis of the current situation shows that there are a few workstations in the nurse's stations with a single printer. No other workstations or printers are available except in offices.

The project scope includes protocol order sets that will be sending orders to pharmacy, laboratory, and radiology systems. It also includes alerts related to the opioid management monitoring program.

Questions

1. What environments would you anticipate you might need?

   For adding new functionality to a current system, typically the existing environments are used, rather that adding any. For this situation, these are the basic environments that would be utilized.
   - Development for all configuration development.
   - Test: to separate the test environment, so any additional configuration does not impact the testing of the system.
   - Training: this will require a large training effort, and the system used should be isolated and should match the training materials.
   - Production

2. Would you anticipate the need for redundancy and disaster recovery for this system?

   Most definitely. This is a critical system for patient care and should be configured with full redundancy and to allow a quick recovery in the event of disaster. With this being new functionality being added to an existing system, it would be good to review the disaster recovery plan and update as needed.

   The current business continuity plan will need to be updated to include how to manage the new functionality when the system is unavailable as well as what information will need to be entered when the system is back available, and by whom.

3. What might be some considerations when evaluating workstations and printers for the end users?

   When evaluating workstations, it is important to understand where the users will be when they need access. With this scenario, the order set functionality, with alerts are being added. These should not change the need for workstation locations if they are already present for order entry. When meeting with the stakeholders, they can be asked about workstations to determine if additional ones are required.

When evaluating printers, the location, physical space, network, and power availability also apply. The analysis of what printing will occur should feed into the quantity needed. Is it the expectation that this is an electronic system and that minimal to no printing will be done? With the new functionality, there may not need to be any additional printing required.

Case Study 2: Implementation of a Research Tracking System

Type: Custom development

Additional Information

Your analysis of the current situation shows that each of the users has access to a computer and printer. Most utilize a personal computer, while a few are using Mac workstations.

It is expected that each user will enter his or her own research data as they are gathered.

Senior leadership would like to see the most current data in the dashboard whenever they log in.

Questions

1. What environments would you anticipate you might need?

   - Sandbox or development: multiple sandbox environments to provide a workspace for each developer, if there are multiple developers. In the case of only one developer, the development environment would work.
   - Test or preproduction: to separate the test environment, so any additional development does not impact the testing of the system.
   - Training could occur in the test/preproduction environment, since there are a limited number of users, and the system should not require ongoing training. This is dependent on the training strategy.
   - Production

2. Would you anticipate the need for redundancy and disaster recovery for this system?

   This is not a critical system, but some redundancy would be beneficial for power and the network if there are concerns over stability. The organization leadership will want to have access when needed and avoid any perception that the system goes down frequently. The disaster recovery plan would include backups of the data for restoration as needed. This would probably be a lower priority for recovery if a disaster strikes.

3. What might be some considerations when evaluating workstations and printers for the end users?

   It appears that all users have access to a workstation. This new system should be built so it is compatible with PC and Mac workstations if both are used in the organization. If the new system is web-based, verifying that it works with multiple browsers should be part of the test plan.

Chapter 10: Security and Privacy

Case Study

Your hospital has decided to shift its scheduling tool to a cloud-based application. Its licensing costs are cheaper than the existing solution and it has more functionality. It will require hosting PHI in the cloud-based solution, data feeds between the application and your EHR. Your internal users and patients will access the tool either via a website or a mobile application.

1. What are the security considerations for hosting PHI in cloud-based tool? What will the access control requirements look like for patient and the hospital user?

   Security considerations for PHI in the cloud are numerous. For starters:
   - Account management—will the system have its own directory service? Or will it integrate with yours?
   - How will auditing/logging be handled? Does the product have tamper proof logs, and are they retained in compliance with HIPAA regulations?
   - Are all encryption requirements met: at rest, and in motion?
   - How efficiently is the vendor handling system patches and application vulnerability maintenance?

- Do they have a functioning disaster recovery and business continuity plan? Is the Incident Response Plan practiced? And does it include notifying you? What are the service level agreements?
- Where is your data actually stored, and is there a detailed reckoning of all parties that have access? Not just to the application, but to all systems that the data traverses or resides in?
- Is your data in a shared database? Or is it segregated into its own instance?
- What is the protocol for retrieving or purging your patient's data in the event the relationship with the vendor ends?

Access control for patient vs. hospital user will obviously need to be very different:

- Patients will likely need "Read Only" access to their appointments, the ability to request changes, and the ability to receive update alerts. You may seek to ensure the system does not require downloading the data before the patient can view it, as a means of keeping it more secure. Optimally, the access includes some form of multifactor authentication, as well as access to the account by a designated "caregiver," in the event the patient is unable to do so.
- Hospital users will require multifactor authentication, as well as role-based access control, which restricts them to the various functions necessary to do their jobs.
- Additionally, the system administrators, or other IT support personnel will need higher levels of system access, with additional levels of control and monitoring.

2. What are the security and privacy controls at the cloud vendor's IT infrastructure? Will the hospital allow access by an Internet-based tool into their EHR? What will need to be considered if the relationship ends?

- Understanding the security and privacy controls on the vendor's infrastructure is essential. They will have access to your patients' PHI; therefore they must meet all HIPAA regulatory obligations. If they do not, and there is a breach, your hospital will still take the reputational hit, even if the vendor becomes financially liable.
- You will need to ensure your executive or risk management teams understand the risks associated with access to your EHR from an Internet-based application. All connections must be secure, the

security team will likely work you through the required necessary controls, and present you with a risk rating, which will need to be signed-off by the leadership team.
  - If the relationship ends, there are a few things that need to be considered:
    • You will need to be able to recover your data/records, in an agreed upon format, and within an agreed upon timeframe.
    • You will also need to recover the audit information that goes along with that data.
    • You will need to understand the protocol with purging or disabling access to your data in the vendor's system. Likely they will not purge, citing their own HIPAA obligations. But it must be rendered inaccessible by their support personnel.
  - Incident response SLA's will need to be maintained for the life of the data in their systems. (Likely seven years beyond the expiration of your contract.)

3. What details are the security team likely to ask you about the solution?

   They are likely to ask you numerous questions related to:
   - Access management and authentication
   - Audit and monitoring capabilities
   - The product's operating environment security, ability to patch, anti-virus, and vulnerability management
   - Network security—firewall rules, white-listing, VPN controls, etc.
   - Remote access and support
   - Incident response capabilities and SLA
   - Encryption in motion and at rest
   - Disaster recovery and business continuity

4. How does this modify the risk assessment for the hospital?

   This solution will definitely introduce a change to the risk assessment. There will be PHI hosted outside your hospital's immediate control, with all the resulting third-party liability concerns.

5. Will you need to develop alternate procedures in the event the Internet, and therefore the tool, are inaccessible?

   Yes, you most definitely will need business continuity or "down time" procedures. You may need to work with your business unit to document how the schedulers will function, if they are unable to reach the tool. If that is not within the scope of the project, it needs to be escalated as a point of concern for others to address.

Chapter 11: Software Testing

Case Study 1: Implementation of an Electronic Health Record

Type: COTS

Additional Information

You have been informed that a group of super users has been identified to assist with the project. They are a combination of nurses and physicians who represent the different patient care areas. They have been involved in redesigning the workflows and developing the requirements. It took a long time to obtain agreement on how the new features will be configured. The IT and vendor staff are now busy with development based on the requirements.

Questions

1. How could you utilize the super users during testing?

   The super users could be involved in identifying the scenarios that feed the test scripts. They could be involved in user acceptance testing, if this is part of the test plan. Depending on their skill set, they could be brought in to assist the test team with integration or system testing.

2. What types of testing would you include with this project/program?

   For a program of this size, unit testing, functional testing, integration testing, system testing, performance testing, and user acceptance testing would all be appropriate. Regression testing will occur after the main test phase, if any modifications or fixes are made, as well as any post-live changes.

3. What types of items would be placed under configuration management?

   Configuration management should be in place for the hardware configuration and software configuration including modifications, updates, and full upgrades. Items that change frequently, such as user accounts, registered workstations, and printers, do not need to be controlled through a configuration management process.

Case Study 2: Implementation of an Organizational Metrics Dashboard

Type: Custom development

Additional Information

You have been informed that a group of super users has been identified to assist with the project. They have been involved in developing the requirements for the new system and are familiar with all data to be collected.

Questions

1. How could you utilize the super users during testing?

   The super users could be involved in providing test data for each of the metrics and assisting with the testing of how the data are loaded. They could be involved in user acceptance testing, if it is part of the test plan. This might not be necessary if they are actively involved in other testing.

2. What types of testing would you include with this project/program?

   For a program of this size, unit testing, functional testing, and system testing would all be appropriate. Regression testing will occur after the main test phase, if any modifications or fixes are made, as well as any post-live changes.

3. What types of items would be placed under configuration management?

   Configuration management should be in place for the software code to include any modifications. Items that change frequently, such as user accounts, do not need to be controlled through a configuration management process.

Chapter 12: Activation Management

Case Study 1: Implementation of an Electronic Health Record

Type: COTS

Additional Information

The activation strategy decision is to go-live with all new functionality in a Big Bang. This will include users in all patient care areas.

Questions

1. What main activities would occur during the activation?

   Pre-activation date
   - Communication.
   - Final setup and configuration of production environment.
   - Adding of interface threads to production—the pharmacy interfaces could be turned on for all new medication.
   - Load of all user accounts—once this is complete, all new user accounts should be added as each request is received.
   - Turn on all system backups, if not completed before.
   - Meeting with support staff to provide a hand-off.
   Activation date
   - Migration of all configuration to the production environment and validation that it was migrated correctly.
   - Turn on production interfaces, if not completed before.
   - Activate all reports.
   - Validate new system prior to turning it over to end users.

2. What level of post-live support should be scheduled?

   This is a change for the users, and it will impact most of the organization. It is recommended that onsite support be provided 24/7 for a week or two, depending on how well they adapt. Schedule for longer than you expect, since it is easier to cancel support staff for the evening and night shifts than to try and schedule them at the last minute based on need. Having staff making rounds through the areas using the new system provides just-in-time training and puts a face to support; both are welcomed by the users. There should also be a method for the users to call when they need help, and no one is around.

Case Study 2: Implementation of a Research Tracking System

Type: Custom development

Additional Information

The activation strategy decision is to go-live with all functionality in a Big Bang. This will include all identified users. It has been requested that the historical data be loaded into the new system.

Questions

1. What main activities would occur during the activation?

    Pre-activation date
    –   Communication
    –   Final setup and configuration of production environment
    –   Migration of all code to the production environment and validation that it was migrated correctly
    –   Load of historical and current research data
    –   Setup of user accounts
    –   Turn on all system backups, if not completed before
    –   Meeting with support staff to provide a hand-off
    Activation date
       If all was prepared ahead of time, the users can just start using the system.

2. How would the activation change if this project was managed using an Agile method?

    The main change would be that the functionality would be activated through releases that occur throughout the project. With each release, the system may be unavailable, depending on how the releases will be applied. Since this is not a critical system, communication should go out to the users regarding when the system will be unavailable. Once the new release is migrated to production, it should be validated to ensure that all changes were correctly made before users are notified that it is available.

3. What level of post-live support should be scheduled?

Providing a method of ongoing communication to the support team may be a sufficient level of support. Scheduling a super user to be with users when they first enter their research data would provide some just-in-time training if necessary, based on how user-friendly the system is.

Chapter 13: Project Transition to Support

Case Study 1: Implementation of an Electronic Health Record

Type: COTS

Additional Information

An organization has decided to replace the EHR. This EHR is a COTS product, provided by a large and well-known vendor, and it will replace a solution that had been used in the hospital for the past decade. The new EHR promises to include a host of new features that were lacking in the original system, such as integration with other hospital systems, new reporting capabilities, and access through mobile devices. Although the hospital has always had its own dedicated IT department, most of the staff has had to acquire new skills, and teams that typically did not have a significant role with the EHR, such as network staff and device management staff, have suddenly become integral to the operations and support of the system. Since the EHR is supplied by an external vendor, there will still be some reliance on the vendor to troubleshoot issues that are beyond the capacity of the internal IT team.

Questions

1. What roles would need to be included in the transition to support?

From the case study, we understand that the IT department would be responsible for the following:

a. Providing configuration of the new COTS system
b. Developing interfaces and integrations with other systems
c. Configuring and deploying mobile devices
d. Providing tier-1 end-user support
e. Escalating tickets to the vendor

Based on those known roles, we can expect that the roles involved in project transition should include the following, at a minimum:

a. Product/process owner—responsible for maintaining the support process, and serves as the escalation point for issues
b. Application administrator—responsible for the day-to-day configuration of the application and helps to escalate tickets to the vendor, as needed
c. Database administrator—responsible for overall system maintenance
d. Desktop/user support—responsible for front-end access methods to the system, which may include mobile devices
e. Systems and networking administrator—responsible for networking, which may include the connections to integrated systems
f. Help desk—responsible for handling tier-1 support requests from customers

It is not clear from the case study whether the application will be hosted on-site or by the vendor, or what the support agreement looks like, but there is the potential to include other roles, such as a server administrator, web administrator, and general operations. Even if these roles are supported directly by the vendor or other contractors, it is important to ensure that everyone in the transition team is aware of how to interact with these groups, if support is needed.

2. What types of documentation would need to be created?

Since this is a new system, all of the documentation described in this chapter are beneficial to include. However, the following types of documentation would be crucial to providing a successful handoff to your support staff from the start:

a. Administrator guide—describes the process of how to configure the system
b. User guide—provides end users with a reference on using the new system
c. Configuration management plan—describes the process for making changes to the system by the application administrators

    d. Knowledge base articles or job aids—guides tier-1 support on how to resolve or route trouble tickets

    e. Service level agreement—specifies how the vendor will provide support to the customer with legal implications

3. How long should the project manager remain involved with the project, post-live?

Despite the significant complexity, duration, and scale of this project, the project manager should still set a specific timetable for exiting the project. If the project adequately prepared supporting staff during the project transition, the project manager should be able to close the project and release resources within two to four weeks. If this duration gets extended, there is a risk that the project manager's role will change to that of a product manager.

Case Study 2: Implementation of an Organizational Metrics Dashboard

Type: Custom development

Additional Information

The PM assigned to the implementation of the metrics dashboard gained a favorable reputation with her customers and colleagues. She has been with the organization for several years and knows who to go to in order to resolve issues. She has the ability to find creative solutions to complex problems and does everything she can to keep things running smoothly, on-time, and on-budget. Being the exceptional PM that she is, she started planning for the transition of the dashboard to the IT department staff early in the project. She ensured that knowledge articles, SOPs, and other reference guides were created and distributed to support staff, whom she refers to as her partners in the project. Since everything was managed so well, the number of issues after go-live was minimal, and the project was closed. Almost a year later, the support center received a call reporting that an executive was unable to access the dashboard to create a monthly report. While the agent tried to help, he was only on the job for a few months and was not familiar with the system and misrouted the ticket. Several hours passed without a response, so the frustrated executive called the PM directly, pleading for help.

Questions

1. How should the PM respond to the customer?

   Despite the history of working closely with the customer, the PM should continue to support the maintenance processes that were developed. The PM can redirect the customer to a manager or supervisor in the support center to try to resolve the problem. In most cases, this will reinforce the processes in place while also allowing the support center to identify training gaps within their own team, thereby strengthening that group even further. If the customer is still unsatisfied, it may be necessary to continue working up the chain of command for that group. However, if the PM simply acknowledges the mistake made by the support agent and agrees to coordinate the right resources herself, she is diminishing the role of the support center and increasing the likelihood that she will be contacted later for a project that has been closed for some time. This can lead to even more problems down the line, since the PM will not be at her desk 24/7 and is less likely to be able to respond as quickly as a properly routed ticket. The problem should be resolved at its source.

2. Who is responsible for training new support staff on existing systems?

   This may vary by organization, but in most cases, it would be the manager of the support staff. There should be a process in place during the onboarding process to help new team members become familiar with the systems that the organization supports and where documentation on those systems can be found. This reinforces the importance of clear, concise, and complete documentation that can be readily accessible by the support teams. There is one thing that is clear, however: the PM should not be responsible for ongoing training of new staff for projects that have been completed and closed.

Chapter 14: Measuring Success

Case Study 1: Implementation of an Electronic Health Record

Type: COTS

Additional Information

Your activation was successful, and the end users are working through the expected workflow issues and trying to remember how to use the system. You have staff providing at-the-elbow assistance to end users to support them during the transition.

Questions

1. What metrics would you use to measure the success of the project implementation itself?

   The project can be measured by any number of criteria. Here is a list of some key areas to evaluate, but the list is not all-inclusive:
   - All patient-related Admission-Discharge-Transfer (ADT) and demographic data were successfully migrated to the new EHR
   - All patient laboratory and radiology data for the past two years have been successfully loaded and are available to the end users
   - The system configuration matches the requirements. This can be split to be specific to orders, results, or clinical documentation criteria. Focus on those requirements believed to be essential by the organization
   - The interfaces are live, match the requirements, and pass the expected data between systems in the expected format
   - The project was completed on time and on budget
   - The hardware arrived on time and was set up and configured according to the plan
   - All end-users attended training and received accounts
   - The activation was completed within the defined timeframe

2. What metrics would you use to measure the success of meeting the strategic objectives?

   The strategic objectives for this project are broader than those for the implementation itself. These systems are implemented to meet organizational goals and should be evaluated to determine if those goals have been met. This may not happen for months after go-live. Metrics could have included a reduction of errors, reduction of duplication of work, improved access to patient information, and improved accuracy of data for patient care decisions. With this in mind, the following could be measured, although this is not an all-inclusive list. When applicable, each metric should include a defined target, so the organization knows when they have met their objectives.

- Medication errors
- Computerized Provider Order Entry (CPOE) use for medication orders
- CPOE use for non-medication orders
- Use of barcode medication administration—compliance rates, and near misses
- Verbal orders count (and rationale)
- Accuracy of heights and weights in the system
- Time spent documenting
- Revenue generated after documentation improvements
- Completion of mandatory documentation (i.e., restraints)
- User satisfaction with system

Case Study 2: Implementation of an Organizational Metrics Dashboard

Type: Custom development

Additional Information

Your activation was successful, and metrics data is starting to be collected and displayed in the new metrics dashboard. Some metrics are not scheduled to be collected for a few months. You had staff providing support during the go-live of the dashboard, and it was appreciated. You have also provided a user's manual for those who might not use the system right away.

Questions

1. What metrics would you use to measure the success of the metrics dashboard project itself?

The project can be measured by any number of criteria. Here is a list of some, although it is not all-inclusive.

- All data sources for the dashboard are accurate
- Historic data needed for the dashboard has been successfully loaded and available
- All data flows appropriately from source systems to the dashboard at the specified time frame (i.e., daily at midnight, hourly, real-time, etc.)
- The system developed matches the requirements. This can be split into the data entry requirements and the dashboard requirements, if desired
- The project was completed on time and on budget
- No additional hardware was required for the project
- All end users attended training (could be on-line) and received appropriate access to the dashboard
- The activation was completed within the defined timeframe
- User satisfaction is acceptable

2. What metrics would you use to measure the success of meeting the strategic objectives?

The strategic objectives for this project could have included an improved method to view and evaluate the ongoing metrics for the organization so that appropriate action can be taken in a timely manner.

These metrics would feed into organizational decisions for patient care and operations. With this in mind, the following could be measured depending on the data displayed in the metrics dashboard (although it is not an all-inclusive list).

- Increased efficiency and productivity of staff who had been previously responsible to gather and assemble the dashboard data, as measured by number of hours spent before and after the use of the new dashboard system
- User satisfaction of the dashboard
- Usability and ease of use of the system
- Number of times dashboard was accessed, and by whom
- Metrics related to the dashboard content. For example, if dashboard data contains wait times in the emergency department, or patient length of stay, or patients with catheters in longer than 48 hours— does the organization see improvements in these measures over time?

Appendix B
Earned Value
Management (EVM)

In alphabetical order

Measurement	Definition	Formula
Actual cost (AC)	The total amount spent on a task up to the current date or total direct and indirect costs from work on an activity during a given period	
Budget at completion (BAC)	The total budget planned at the end of the project	
Cost performance index (CPI)	The ratio of earned value to actual cost. This ratio is used to estimate the projected cost of completing the project. If the CPI equals 1, the actual costs are equal to the budget. If the CPI is less than 1, the actual costs are over budget. If the CPI is greater than 1, the actual costs are under budget.	CPI = EV/AC

Measurement	Definition	Formula
Cost variance (CV)	The difference between the work that has been accomplished (in dollars) and how much was spent to accomplish it	$CV = EV - AC$
Earned value (EV)	The budgeted cost of work completed as of the current date and is based on the planned costs and the rate the team is completing the work to date	$EV = PV$ to date $\times RP$
Estimate at completion (EAC)	A forecast of total costs that will be accrued by project completion based on past cost performance trends. There are multiple formulas that can be used to calculate the EAC	$EAC = BAC/CPI$ $EAC = EAC - AC$ $EAC = AC + ((BAC - EV)/CPI)$
Estimate to completion (ETC)	The estimate to complete the remaining work of the project, based on objective measures.	$ETC = EAC - AC$
Percent complete	The progress to completion of a task and it is related as either EV/BAC, or simply the physical progress toward completion. If formal earned value measurements are not required, this value is often estimated by the task resource.	
Planned value (PV)	The portion of the total estimated costs to be spent on an activity during a given period	

Rate of performance (RP)	The ratio of actual work completed to the percent of work planned to have been completed at any given time	RP = Actual work/ Planned work
Schedule performance index (SPI)	The ratio of earned value to planned value. This ratio is used to estimate the projected time to completion of the project. The outcome is similar to the CPI. If the SPI equals 1, the project is on schedule. If the SPI is less than 1, the project is behind schedule. If the SPI is greater than 1, the project is ahead of schedule.	SPI = EV/PV
Schedule variance (SV)	The difference between what was planned to be completed and what has actually been completed as of a specific date	SV = EV – PV
To-complete performance index (TCPI)	Indicates the CPI required throughout the remainder of the project to stay within the stated budget	TCPI = (BAC – EV)/ (BAC – AC)
Variance at completion (VAC)	The variance between the original planned value and the new estimate at completion	VAC = BAC – EAC

Appendix C
Forms and Templates

Template #1: Initiation Worksheet

This is a worksheet to help in the gathering of information in the Project Initiation Phase.

***Project Name**:*

***Project Manager**:*

Business Need:

Goals and Objectives:

■

Deliverables:

■

Stakeholders:

■

Constraints:

■

Assumptions:

■

Relevant Historical Information:

Resource Needs:

■

Template #2: Communication Management Plan

Who	What	When	How	Responsible

Template #3: Communication Management Plan

Basic Communication Plan—*add rows as needed*

Name/Audience/ Role	What Info is Needed?	When is the Info Needed?	Vehicle/Method for Reporting	Responsible Party
	•	•	•	
	•	•	•	
	•	•	•	

Stakeholder Analysis—*add rows as needed*

Who will be Impacted by this Project?	Will or How will they Contribute to the Project?	Focus (Internal vs. External)	What is this Person's/ Group's Interest in the Project?	Are they Supportive, Neutral or Opposed?	What can be done to Change those who are Opposed to Neutral or Supportive?

Communication Vehicles—*add rows as needed*

Method	Contact or Responsible Party	Used for this Project?
Newsletter		
Flyers/Brochures		
Mass Email Notifications		
Stakeholder Briefings		

Template #4: Project Charter

Executive Summary

<Document an executive summary of the project>

Project Scope

Goals and Objectives:

- <List of Goals and Objectives>

In Scope

- <List of what is in scope>

Out of Scope

- <List of what is out of scope>

Key Success Factors

Description	Target	Minimum Acceptable

Project Structure and Administration

Roles and Responsibilities:
(Include all project team members; assure commitment of time from appropriate manager; communicate roles to team members)

Role	Name	Description
		•
		•

Issues Management Approach:
<Describe how issues will be identified and managed>

Change Control Guidelines:
<Describe how project changes will be identified, managed, and approval authority>

Communication Plan
<Describe the communication plan to set expectations>

Risk Management Plan
<Describe how risks will be identified and managed>

Project Approach

Major Phases and Stages
  1. <Briefly define scope of each phase or stage>

Deliverables:
  1. <List all deliverables>

Related Dependent Projects:
  ■ <List any related or dependent projects and relationship>

Other:
<Define anything else that is significant about this project>

Charter Sign-Off Sheet

Role	Name	Signature
Business Representative		
IT Administration		
IT Project Manager		

Appendix A: Project Work-plan

Appendix B: Project Assumptions

Appendix C: Project Budget

Template #5: Project Charter

\<Project Title\>

Project Charter

\<Version/Draft\>

Date

Prepared By:

Table of Contents

1 **Profile** 227

2 **Purpose of Charter** 227

3 **Background** 227

4 **Objectives** 227

5 **High Level Scope** 227

6 **Project Description and Major Deliverables** 227

7 **Critical Measurements** 227

8 **Success Factors** 227

9 **Stakeholders** 228

10 **Cost Management** 228

11 **Project Documentation** 228

12 **Communication Plan** 228

13 **Project Planning** 228

14 **Issue Management/Decision Tracking** 228

15 **Risk Management** 228

16 **Project Closeout** 228

1. Profile

1.1 Project ID:
1.2 Project Name:
1.3 Project Type:
1.4 Business Group:
1.5 This Project Charter has been delivered, reviewed, and approved, as shown below:

Stakeholder Name	Role	Dept./Area	Signatures	Date

1.6 Estimated Start Date:
1.7 Estimated Finish Date:
1.8 Business Need and Core Benefits:
<Why are we doing this project?>

2. Purpose of Charter

3. Background

4. Objectives

5. High Level Scope

6. Project Description and Major Deliverables

7. Critical Measurements

8. Success Factors

9. Stakeholders

Role	Name	Responsibility/Title

10. Cost Management

11. Project Documentation

Project Document	Owned By	Purpose	Frequency

12. Communication Plan

13. Project Planning

14. Issue Management/Decision Tracking

15. Risk Management

16. Project Closeout

Template #6: Project Scope

Mission Statement:

Project Objectives:

- ■

Project Justification

Leadership Roles:

    Sponsor:
    Project Manager:
    Project Leaders:
    Project Resources:

Project Milestones:

    <u>Milestone</u>   <u>Estimated Completion Date</u>

Measures of Success:

- ■

Assumptions:

- ■

Constraints:

- ■

_____   _____

Sponsor   Date

Template #7: Project Scope

***Goal**:*

***Project Objectives/Scope**:*

   ■

Project Justification:

Project Team:

Role	Name	Contact Information
Project Sponsor(s)		
Project Manager		
Project Team Resources		

Implementation Strategy:

Training Strategy:

Communication Plan:

Audience	What	How	When	Responsible Party

Risk Assessment:

Risk –
Mitigation –

Risk –
Mitigation –

Project Milestones:

<u>Milestone</u>   <u>Estimated Completion Date</u>

Measures of Success:

■

Assumptions:

■

Constraints:

■

_____   _____

Project Sponsor   Date

Template #8: Project Roles and Contacts

Last Updated: <Date>

Role (Organization)	Name	Phone	E-mail
Project Manager			
Sponsor			
Contract Officer			
Workflow Analysis and Design			
Integration			
Development/Configuration			
Training			
Technical Lead			

Role (Vendor/Contractor)	Name	Phone	E-mail
Project Manager			
Workflow Analysis and Design			
Integration Resource			
Technical Resource			
Training Resource			

Template #9: Agile Roadmap

Agile Roadmap Template

	Q1	Q2	Q3	Q4
Release	Release 1		Release 2	
Sprint				
Features	🗒️ 🗒️	🗒️ 🗒️	🗒️ 🗒️ 🗒️	🗒️ 🗒️
Epics	🗒️	🗒️	🗒️	
User Stories	🗒️ 🗒️ 🗒️	🗒️ 🗒️ 🗒️	🗒️ 🗒️	🗒️ 🗒️ 🗒️

Template #10: Agile Requirements Management Plan

Agile Requirements Management Plan

1. Executive Summary
Provide a summary of the project

2. Purpose
Provide the purpose of this document related to the project

3. Roadmap
Provide an explanation of the roadmap, what it is, and how it will be utilized for this project.

4. User Story
Provide an explanation of user stories and how they will be utilized for this project.

5. Epic
Provide an explanation of epics and how they will be utilized for this project.

6. Product Backlog
Provide an explanation of the product backlog and how they will be utilized for this project.

7. Feature
Provide an explanation of a feature and how they will be used for this project.

8. The User Story Template
When documenting user stories, there are specific characteristics that should be used. These follow the **INVEST** acronym

Independent	The user story should not be sequential or locked into a specific order.
Negotiable	The user story should be flexible and without too much detail.
Valuable	The user story should add value to the final product.
Estimable	The user story should be written so that the team can estimate the level of effort.
Small	The user story should be able to be designed, built, and tested within a single iteration.
Testable	The user story should be able to be tested with some type of acceptance criteria or other test (even if it has not yet been defined).

The *<organization name>* has a template to assist with documenting the user story.

Template #11: Agenda-Minutes

Purpose:
Date and Time:
Location:
Facilitator:

Invited:	Attended?	Invited:	Attended?

Topics

Action Items	Responsible Parties

Template #12: User Story

User Story Template

Project:
Project Manager:
User Story ID:
User Story Name:
Related Epic #:
Related Feature #:
User Story Background:
Assumptions:
Roles and Privileges:

Role	Description	Create	Read	Update	Delete
Administrator					
End User					
Customer Service					
Other?					

Acceptance Criteria:
    Acceptance Criteria # 1
    Given
    When
    Then

    Acceptance Criteria # 2
    Given
    When
    Then

    Acceptance Criteria # 3
    Given
    When
    Then

Template #13: Project Status Report

Project:

Project Manager:

Reporting Date:

Overall Status: _____ *(Green, Yellow, Red)* **Reason for Yellow or Red Status:** **Risk and Impact:**	**Accomplishments:** **Kudos:**
Issues/Resolution Plan: •	
Next Steps:	
Other:	

Template #14: Project Status Report

PM:

Reporting Date:

Significant Issues/Risks:

■

Accomplishments:

■

Next Scheduled Tasks

■

EVM Measurements

■

Template #15: Options Document

Delete upon completion of document: Add or remove rows based on the necessary information for a decision. Always include first three rows. Add or remove columns based on the number of options to be evaluated.

Description of Issue/Problem:

Assumptions/Constraints:

Recommendation and Why:

	Option 1	*Option 2*	*Option 3*	*Options 4*
Description:	•	•	•	•
Advantages:	•	•	•	•
Disadvantages:	•	•	•	•
Estimated Cost:	•	•	•	•
Estimated Resources:	•	•	•	•
Estimated Duration:	•	•	•	•
Impact to Workflow:	•	•	•	•
Impact to Dataflow:	•	•	•	•
Risks:	•	•	•	•
Barriers/Challenges	•	•	•	•
Other:	•	•	•	•

Template #16: Project Scope Change

CHANGE REQUEST

Project: _____   **Change #:** _____

Date Submitted: _____   **Submitted By:** _____

Short Description of Change: *(for reporting purposes)*

Criticality: _____

Criticality LEGEND:
1 - *"Showstopper"; must be done; no alternatives*
2 - *Immediate need; workarounds not preferred*
3 - *Immediate need; workarounds are acceptable*
4 - *Phased; no workarounds - can be done at a later date*
5 - *Phased; workarounds exist - can be done at a later date*
6 - *Not Urgent; "nice to have"*

Detailed Description of Change:

Possible Workarounds: *(List possible alternative solutions if change is not approved)*

Justification: *(Why this change is being requested)*

Impact if Change Not Accepted: *(List all areas impacted if change is not approved)*

IMPACT ANALYSIS

To be completed by Project Team

Project: _____   **Change #:** _____

Short Description of Change:

Impact of Change Requested: *(List all impacts to project)*

Impact to Other Projects or Systems:
Impact to Human Resources:
Impact to Other Resources:
Impact to Project Timeline:
Other:

Detailed Description of Work Required to Complete Request: *(Include all tasks required)*

Approval Status:

Approve: Deny: Defer to _____:

When

Approval Signatures:

_____   _____
Project Manager   *Date*

_____   _____
Project Sponsor   *Date*

Template #17: Change Request

Change Request

To be completed by Requestor

Project: **Date Submitted:**

Submitted By: **Change #:**

Description of Change:

Justification:

Possible Workarounds:

IMPACT ANALYSIS

To be completed by Project Team

Impact of Change Requested: *(List all impacts to project)*

Impact to Other Projects or Systems:	
Impact to Human Resources:	
Impact to Other Resources:	
Impact to Project Timeline:	
Other:	

Detailed Description of Work Required to Complete Request:
(Include all tasks required)

Approval Status

To be completed by Project Manager and Sponsors

Approve: Deny: Defer to *(when)*:

Approval Signature:

_____   _____

Project Sponsor   *Date*

Template #18: Operational Readiness Review (ORR)

Operational Readiness Review

Category	Readiness Criteria	Scheduled Completion Date	Actual Completion Date	Responsible Party	% Compl	Status/ Comments/ Concerns
Management						
Hardware and Architecture						
Development and Configuration						
User Access and User Security						
Data Migration						
System Security and Pivacy						
Training						
Training						
Configuration Management Process						
Post-Live Support						
User Department						

Template #19: Activation Checklist

<Project Name> Activation (Go-live) Checklist

All activation procedures can be found here: \\sapphire\CRISshare\PMO Projects\Project Name\Activation

X	#	Task	Est Duration	Est Start	Actual Start	Est Finish	Actual Finish	Predecessor	Resource	Comment
				X Weeks Before Go-Live						
	1									
	2									
	3									
				Week of Go-Live						
	4									
	5									
	6									
				Activation Day						
	7	Communication								
		System Down								
	8	Existing Task								
	9	Task Added During Activation								
	10									
	11									
	12									
		System Up								
	13	Communication								
				Post Go-Live Support						
	14									
	15									

Template #20: Post-live Issue Template

4.5 Upgrade
Post-Live Issues

#	Issue Name	Description	Current Status	Comment/Update	Resp. Party

Template #21: Lessons Learned

[Name of Project] Lessons Learned

[Insert summary of the project implementation and activation, including the date when the project was activated.] The identified areas of success and improvement are listed below, and sorted into pre-Activation, Activation, and post-Activation.

Pre-Activation

Successes:

1.
2.
3.

Areas for Improvement:

4.
5.
6.

Activation

Successes:

7.
8.
9.

Areas for Improvement:

10.
11.
12.

Post-Activation:

Successes:

13.
14.
15.

Areas for Improvement:

16.
17.
18.

Template #22: Project Completion Analysis Document

Project Goal:

Project Sponsor:

Project Manager:

Project Objectives/Scope:

- ■ <Objective and If Met>

Measures of Success/Expected Outcomes:

- ■ <Measurement and Outcomes/results>

Implementation Strategy:
<Strategy and if followed, or change and why>

Risk Impact:

Risk –
Mitigation –

Update: *<Any update on risk, if appeared and how it was mitigated>*

Constraints:

- ■ <Constraints and any comments/feedback>

Major Project Milestones:

Milestone	Est. Compl. Date	Actual Compl. Date

<Include any comments on the milestones>

Lessons Learned:

Project Success:

- ■

Areas for Improvement:

- ■

Sponsor Comments:

_____   _____

Sponsor   Date

Template #23: Project Completion Document

Mission Statement:
[Can be copied from Scope Document]

Project Sponsors: [Can be copied from Scope Document]
Project Managers: [Can be copied from Scope Document]

Project Scope/Objectives:
[Can be copied from Scope Document. Include any Phases of development. Include whether or not the objectives were met. Add any Scope Changes, which were done as Objectives.]

Measures of Success/Expected Outcomes:
[Can be copied from Scope Document. Include whether or not they were met.]

Implementation Strategy:
[Can be copied from Scope Document. Include whether this was followed without modification or any changes, which were made to the strategy.]

Scope Changes:
[Include Scope Changes, which were not accepted into the project.]

Risk Impact:
Risk –
Mitigation –
[Can be copied from Scope Document. Include the outcome of the risk.]

Constraints:
[Can be copied from Scope Document. Include the outcome of the Constraints]

Outstanding Issues:
[Include issues, which were not resolved during the project period, and the disposition of these items.]

Major Project Milestones (Phase I):

<u>Milestone</u>   <u>Estimated Completion Date</u>   <u>Actual Completion Date</u>

[Can be copied from Scope Document. Include the changes to the Milestone dates and reasons that the dates changed.]

Lessons Learned:
[Created from the Lessons Learned meeting after Project Go Live.]

Sponsor Comments:

_____   _____

Sponsor –   Date

_____   _____

Sponsor –   Date

References and Additional Readings

Books

Aiello B, Sachs L. Configuration Management Best Practices. Boston: Addison Wesley; 2010.

HIMSS. HIMSS Dictionary of Health Information and Technology Terms, Acronyms and Organizations 5th ed. Boca Raton: CRC Press; 2019

Houston, S., Kennedy, R. 'Effective Lifecycle Management of Healthcare Applications: Achieving Best Practices by Using a Portfolio Framework (HIMSS Series)', Boca Raton: CRC Press; 2020.

Project Management Institute. Agile Practice Guide. Newtown Square, PA: Project Management Institute; 2017.

Project Management Institute. A Guide to the Project Management Body of Knowledge. (PMBOK®) 6th ed. Newtown Square, PA: Project Management Institute; 2017.

Project Management Institute. The Standard for Portfolio Management. 4th ed. Newtown Square, PA: Project Management Institute; 2017.

Schiesser R. IT Systems Management 2nd ed. Boston: Prentice Hall; 2010.

Schwalbe K. Information Technology Project Management 8th ed. Cambridge, MA: Course Technology; 2016.

Websites

The Agency for Healthcare Research and Quality (www.ahrq.org)
American Health Quality Association (www.ahqa.org)
Agile Manifesto (https://agilemanifesto.org/history.html)
American Nursing Informatics Association (www.ania.org)
American Medical Informatics Association (www.amia.org)
FDA Medical Device Cybersecurity Guidance (https://www.fda.gov/medical-devices/digital-health-center-excellence/cybersecurity)

FDA Document – Postmarket Management of Cybersecurity in Medical Devices Guidance for Industry and Food and Drug Administration Staff, Document issued on December 28, 2016 (http://www.fda.gov/downloads/MedicalDevices/DeviceRegulationandGuidance/GuidanceDocuments/UCM482022.pdf)

Federal Information Security Management Act of 2002 (http://csrc.nist.gov/groups/SMA/fisma/)

Federal Information Security Modernization Act of 2014 (https://www.dhs.gov/fisma)

Health & Human Services Office for Civil Rights (OCR) Breach Portal (https://ocrportal.hhs.gov/ocr/breach/breach_report.jsf)

Health and Human Services, Health Information Privacy site (https://www.hhs.gov/hipaa)

Healthcare Information and Management Systems Society (www.himss.org)

The HIPAA Privacy Rule (https://www.hhs.gov/hipaa/for-professionals/privacy/index.html)

Institute for Healthcare Improvement (www.ihi.org)

The Joint Commission (www.jointcommission.org)

Leapfrog Group (www.leapfroggroup.org)

National Association for Healthcare Quality (www.nahq.org)

National Committee for Quality Assurance (www.ncqa.org)

National Institute of Standards and Technology (www.nist.gov)

Updated NIST Software Uses Combination Testing to Catch Bugs Fast and Easy, November 9, 2010 (https://www.nist.gov/news-events/news/2010/11/updated-nist-software-uses-combination-testing-catch-bugs-fast-and-easy)

The National Quality Forum (www.qualityforum.org)

Office of the National Coordinator for Health Information Technology (https://www.healthit.gov)

Office of the National Coordinator for Health Information Technology 10-year Vision for Health Information Exchange (https://www.healthit.gov/resource/10-year-vision-achie-ve-interoperable-health-it-infrastructure)

Office of the National Coordinator for Health Information Technology (ONC) Safety Assurance Factors for HER Resilience (SAFER) guides (https://www.healthit.gov/safer/safer-guides)

FDA Document – Postmarket Management of Cybersecurity in Medical Devices Guidance for Industry and Food and Drug Administration Staff, Document issued on December 28, 2016 (http://www.fda.gov/downloads/MedicalDevices/DeviceRegulationandGuidance/GuidanceDocuments/UCM482022.pdf)

Principles Behind the Agile Manifesto (https://www.agilealliance.org/agile101/12-principles-behind-the-agile-manifesto/)

Project Management Institute (www.pmi.org)

Index

Italicized and **bold** pages refer to figures and tables respectively

A

Access management and authentication, 125
Activation, 146–148
Activation checklist, 148–150
   template, 244
Activation management, 143–154
   case study(ies)
      EHR implementation, 154, 206–207
      research tracking system, 154, 207–208
   user training, 144
Activation planning, 153
Activation rehearsal, 150–153
Administrator guide, **169**
Agency for Healthcare Research and Quality (AHRQ), 178
   Health Information Technology Evaluation Toolkit, 176–177
Agenda-minutes, template, 235
Agile development methodology, 63–70
   Agile methods, 65–66
   Agile mindset, 64–65
   levels of planning, 69, *69*
   life cycle selection, 66–67
   practices and terms, 67–69
      backlog, 68
      burndown chart, 68
      burnup chart, 68
      daily standups, 68
      demonstrations, 68
      epic, 68

      release, 68
      retrospectives, 67–68
      reviews, 68
      sprints, 68
      user story, 68
   principles, 64–65
   SDLC, 57–58
Agile life cycle, 67
Agile Manifesto, 63, 64, 70n1, 70n2
Agile method(s), 1, 53, 65–66, 75–77, **87**; *see also* Agile development methodology
   advantages, 76
   disadvantages, 76–77
   DSDM, 66, 75
   Extreme Programming (XP), 66, 75
   Feature Driven Development (FDD), 66, 75
   Kaban method, 65–66, 75
   Lean method, 65, 75
   levels of planning, 69, *69*
   Scrum Framework, 65, 75
Agile mindset, 64–65
Agile requirements management plan, template, 234
Agile roadmap, template, 233
American Health Quality Association, 178
Analyst, **166**
Application administrator, **165**
Audit, 125
Authentication, 125

255

B

Backlog, 68
Backup, 111
BIA, *see* Business impact assessment
Budget, 24, 84
Burndown chart, 68
Burnup chart, 68
Business, project management methodology
    selection and, 80–81
  culture, 81
  discipline, 81
  flexibility, 81
  industry, 80–81
  legal issues, 81
  organization, 80
  resources, 81, 83
Business continuity and disaster recovery, 126
Business impact assessment (BIA), 168, **169**

C

Case study(ies)
  EHR system implementation, 15, 88–89,
    181–182, 191–193
    activation management, 154, 206–207
    knowledge areas, 48–49, 186–188
    process groups, 30, 183–184
    project transition to support, 171,
      208–210
    SDLC, 60, 189–190
    software testing, 141–142, 204–205
    success measurement, 179, 212–213
    system configuration, 118–119,
      198–200
  feedback, 181–214
  organizational metrics dashboard
    implementation, 193–194
    knowledge areas, 49, 188–189
    project transition to support, 171–172,
      210–211
    SDLC, 61, 190–191
    software testing, 141–142, 205
    success measurement, 179–180,
      213–214
  research tracking system implementation,
    15–16, 182–183

  activation management, 154, 207–208
  process groups, 30, 185–186
  system configuration, 119, 200–201
  system access by outside resources, 131,
    201–204
Change management, 159
Change management plan, 25
Change request, template, 242
Client, 108–109
Closing process group, 18, 29–30
Commercial off-the-shelf (COTS) system,
    1–2, 38, 40–41, 58–60, 74, 76,
    134, 141
Committees, 93
Communication, 44
  risks and, 45–46
Communication management, 44–45
Communication management plan, 24–
    25, 26
  templates, 221–222
Communication plan, 44
  stakeholder management, 99–103, **100**
Complexity, 84–85
Computer-based training (CBT), 144
Computerized provider order entry (CPOE)
    system, 174, 176
Computers on wheels (COWs), 113
Configuration and change management, 2
Configuration management, 126, 139–141
Configuration management plan, 140, **169**
Constraints, 85; *see also* Risk(s)
Contracting, 47
Cost(s), 41–42
  management, 41–42
  non-project related, 161
  for software development, 42
  total cost of ownership (TCO), 160
COTS system, *see* Commercial off-the-shelf
    system
Crystal, Dynamic Systems Development
    Method (DSDM), 66, 75
Culture, 81
Custom-developed software, 1, 2
Customers, project methodology selection
    and, 81–83
Cybersecurity, 123–124, 134
  testing, 139

D

Daily standups, 68
Database administrator, **165**
Data security, 126
Demilitarization zone (DMZ), 113
Demonstrations, 68
Department-specific systems, 127, 128
Desktop/user support, **166**
Development lifecycle, 2
Development phase, SDLC, 51, 53–54
Disaster recovery, 110–112
Disaster recovery plan, 111
Discipline, 81

E

Earned value management (EVM), 28, 174,
         215–217
Electronic health record (EHR) system, 11,
         112, 114
    implementation (case studies), 15,
         181–182, 191–193
        activation management, 154, 206–207
        knowledge areas, 48–49, 186–188
        process groups, 30, 183–184
        project transition to support, 171,
         208–210
        SDLC, 60, 189–190
        software testing, 141–142, 204–205
        stakeholder management, 104, 194–196
        success measurement, 179, 212–213
        system configuration, 118–119,
         198–200
    vendors, 129
End-users, 93
Environment(s), 115–118
    considerations, 117–118
    development, 116
    positive customer support, 158
    preproduction, 117
    production, 117
    sandbox, 115
    test, 116
    training, 117
Epic, 68
Escalation process, 158

EVM, *see* Earned value management
Executing process group, 17, 26–27
Executive leadership, 92
Executive leadership owner, **165**
External resources, 93
Extreme Programming (XP), 66, 75

F

Feature Driven Development (FDD), 66, 75
Federal Information Security Management
         Act (FISMA), 123–124
Flexibility, 81
Frequently asked questions (FAQs), 138,
         144, 145
Full backup, 111
Functional/department managers, 93
Functional testing, 135

G

General manager, 6
General operations, **166**
Graphical user interface (GUI), 113

H

Hardware, initiating process groups, 20
Healthcare quality and safety, 178
Health information exchange (HIE), 129
Health Information Portability and
         Accountability Act (HIPAA) Security
         Rule, 123, 124
Health Level 7 (HL7), 114
Help desk, 153, **166**
HHS Security Risk Assessment, 130
High availability, 112
HIPAA Business Associates Agreement
         (BAA), 127
HIPAA Security Rule, 130
How-to quick reference guide, **169**
Human resources, 20
Hybrid life cycle, 67
Hybrid method, 77–79, **88**
    advantages, 78
    disadvantages, 78–79
    format, 77–78

I

Incident response, 126
Incremental life cycle, 67
Incremental model, 57
Industry, 80–81
Information technology (IT), 7, 159
    investment, 174
    projects, 41
    systems, 121
Initiating process group, 17, 19–21
    hardware, 20
    project charter, 20, 21
    project objectives, 20
    questions, 19–20
    resources needed, 20
    software, 20
Initiation worksheet, template, 220
Institute for Healthcare Improvement, 178
Integration management, 33, 37–38
Interface, 113–115
Iterative life cycle, 67
IT projects, security and privacy tasks,
        124–130

J

Job aids, 167
Joint Commission, 178

K

Kaban method, 65–66, 75
Kick-off meeting, 25
Knowledge areas, 33–49
    case study(ies)
        electronic health record
            implementation, 48–49, 186–188
        organizational metrics dashboard
            implementation, 49, 188–189
    communication management, 44–45
    cost management, 41–42
    integration management, 33, 37–38
    and process groups, relationship
        between, 33, **34–36**
    procurement management, 47–48
    project stakeholder management, 48

    quality management, 42–43
    resource management, 43–44
    risk management, 45–46
    schedule management, 39–41
    scope management, 38–39
Knowledge base articles (KBAs), 167, **169**

L

Leadership, executive, 92
Lean method, 65, 75
Leapfrog Group, 178
Legal issues, 81
Life cycle
    agile, 67
    hybrid, 67
    incremental, 67
    iterative, 67
    predictive, 66
    selection, 66–67

M

Malicious code, protection from, 125–126
Memorandum of understanding (MoU), 127,
        164, **170**
Methodology, **86–88**
    case study(ies)
        electronic health record
            implementation, 88–89
        organizational metrics dashboard
            implementation, 89–90
    characteristics, 73–79
        Agile, 75–77, **87**
        hybrid, 77–79, **88**
        waterfall, 73–75, **86**
    defined, 71–72
    selection
        business and, 80–81
        culture, 81
        discipline, 81
        factors to consider, 79–86
        flexibility, 81
        importance of, 72–73
        industry, 80–81
        legal issues, 81
        organization, 80

project characteristics and, 83–86
resources, 81
stakeholders, customers, and
resources, 81–83
Metrics, support center, 158
Micro-management, 6
Mobile devices, 108
Monitoring, 125
and controlling process group, 17–18,
27–28
Multiple thin clients, 109

N

National Association for Healthcare, 178
National Committee for Quality
Assurance, 178
National Institute of Standards and
Technology, 134
National Quality Forum, 178
National Resource Center, 177
Network(s), 112–113
Network security, 126
Non-functional testing, 137

O

Office of the National Coordinator for
Health Information Technology
(ONC), 129
ONC Safety Assurance Factors for
EHR Resilience (SAFER) self-
assessment, 130
Operational readiness review (ORR),
template of, 243
Operations and maintenance (O&M),
9–10, 133
Operations *vs.* project, 9–10
Opportunity and risks, balance between,
46
Options document, 239
Organization, 80
Organizational metrics dashboard
implementation (case studies), 193–194
knowledge areas, 49, 188–189
organizational metrics dashboard
implementation, 89–90

project transition to support, 171–172,
210–211
SDLC, 61, 190–191
software testing, 142, 205
success measurement, 179–180, 213–214
Organizations, 3
Outcome measurement, 175–176; *see also*
Success measurement
Outcomes evaluation plan, 177–178
Outsourcing, 47

P

PACS, *see* Picture archiving and
communication system
Parallel testing, 138–139, 145
Payment Card Information (PCI), 121, 122
PCI, *see* Payment Card Information
PDMP, *see* Prescription drug monitoring
program
Performance testing, 137–138
Personal health record (PHR), 127
Personally Identifiable Information (PII),
121, 122
PHI, *see* Protected health information (PHI)
Picture archiving and communication
system (PACS), 108
PII, *see* Personally Identifiable Information
(PII)
Planning
for activation, 2
levels, Agile method, 69, *69*
project transition to support, 163–165
Planning process group, 17, 22–26
budget, 24
change management plan, 25
communication management plan, 24–25
custom reports, 23
kick-off meeting, 25
project management plan, 22–24
project scope document, 23
project sponsor, 25
risk management plan, 22, 24
scope management plan, 24
PMO, *see* Project management office
Portfolio, 11–12, *12*
Portfolio management, 5, 10–13

vs. program management, **14**
vs. project management, 14
Portfolio manager, goal of, 12
Positive customer support, 158
Post-live issue template, 245
Post-live Project Documentation, **169–170**
Predictive life cycle, 66
Preproduction, 117
Prescription drug monitoring program
       (PDMP), 11, 15
Privacy Act of 1974, 123
Process groups, 17–31
    case study(ies), 30–31
       electronic health record, 30, 183–184
       research tracking system, 31, 185–186
    closing, 18, 29–30
    executing, 17, 26–27
    initiating, 17, 19–21
       hardware, 20
       project charter, 20, 21
       project objectives, 20
       questions, 19–20
       resources needed, 20
       software, 20
    and knowledge areas, relationship
       between, 33, **34–36**
    monitoring and controlling, 17–18, 27–28
    overview, 17–18, *18*
    phases, 17–18, *18*
    planning, 17, 22–26
       budget, 24
       change management plan, 25
       communication management plan,
          24–25
       custom reports, 23
       kick-off meeting, 25
       project management plan, 22–24
       project scope document, 23
       project sponsor, 25
       risk management plan, 22, 24
       scope management plan, 24
Procurement, 83
Procurement management, 47–48
Procurement planning, 47
Product development, **166**
Production environment, 117
Product life cycle, 85

Product manager, 158–159
Product owner, 161, **165**
    roles, 161–162
Product(s)
    defined, 4
    unique, 4, *5*
Program, 10, 11–12, *12*
Program management, 5, 10–13
    vs. portfolio management, **14**
    process groups, *see* Process groups
    vs. project management, 14
Program management office, 13
Program managers, 11
    role, 11–12
    skills, 11
    stakeholders, 94–95
Project charter, 20, 21
    contents, 21
    template, 223–228
Project completion analysis document,
       template of, 248–249
Project completion document, template of,
       250–251
Project development, 4
Project lifecycle, 40
Project management, 3, 5–8, 13
    benefits of, 12
    defined, 6
    methodology, *see* Methodology
    vs. portfolio management, **14**
    vs. program management, **14**
    tools, 85
Project Management Institute (PMI), 33
Project management office (PMO), 12–13,
       21, 155
    benefits, 13
    features, 13
Project management plan, 22–24
Project manager(s), 2, 83, 93
    key skills, 6–7, **7**
    roles, 6
Project portfolio office, 13
Project(s), 3–5, 11–12, *12*
    budget, 84
    characteristics, method selection and,
       84–86
    complexity, 84–85

defined, 3–4
duration, 3–4
IT projects security and privacy tasks,
    124–130
methodology, *see* Methodology
vs. operations, 9–10
outcome, 4
outcome measurement, 175–176
product life cycle, 85
requirements and design, 4
risks and constraints, 85
scope, 84
team, 4
timeline, 84
tools, 85
unique product, 4, 5
Project scope change, template of,
    240–241
Project scope document, 23
    template of, 229–231
Project sponsor(s), 25, 29, 92
Project stakeholder management, *see*
    Stakeholder management
Project status report, template of, 237–238
Project summary and reference document,
    170
Project team, 83, 93
Project transition, to support, 155–172
    case study(ies)
        EHR implementation, 171, 208–210
        organizational metrics dashboard
            implementation, 171–172, 210–211
    change management, 159
    closing, 168–170
    execution, 167–168
    initiating, 160–162
    management, throughout plan, 160
    planning, 163–165
    post-live project documentation,
        169–170
    roles and responsibilities, **165–166**
    scenario, 156–157
    support center
        characteristics, 157–158
        environment of positive customer
            support, 158
        escalation process, 158

metrics, 158
        product manager, 158–159
        resources, 158
        strive for first call resolution, 158
Protected health information (PHI), 121,
    122
Public-facing websites, 127
Purchasing, 47

Q

Quality
    defined, 42
    measuring, 43
Quality management, 42–43
Quality planning process, 42

R

Rapid prototype model, 56–57
Redundancy, 112
Regression testing, 137
Release, 68
Release management, 141
Remote access and support, 126
Request for proposal (RFP), 47
Research tracking system
    implementation (case studies), 15–16,
        182–183
        activation management, 154, 207–208
        process groups, 31
        stakeholder management, 104–105,
            196–198
        system configuration, 118–119,
            200–201
Resource management, 43–44
Resources, 81, 83
    defined, 83
    external, 93
    support center, 158
Retrospectives, 67–68
Reviews, 68
Risk-adverse organization, 46
Risk analysis, 46
Risk management, 45–46
Risk management plan, 22, 24, 27
Risk mitigation, 46

Risk(s), 85
  communication of, 45–46
  identification, 27, 45
  and opportunity, balance between, 46
  probability of, 46

S

SAFER Guides, 130
Sample test script, **136**
SAN, *see* Storage area network (SAN)
Sandbox environment, 115
Schedule management, 39–41
Scope, defined, 38
Scope, project, *see* Project scope
Scope creep, 28
Scope management, 38–39
Scope management plan, 24
Scrum Framework, 65, 75
SDLC, *see* Software development lifecycle
    (SDLC)
Security and privacy, 2, 121–131
  access management and authentication,
    125
  audit and monitoring, 125
  business continuity and disaster
    recovery, 126
  configuration management, 126
  data security, 126
  incident response, 126
  IT projects, 124–130
  network security, 126
  protection from malicious code, 125–126
  remote access and support, 126
  system access by outside resources (case
    study), 131, 201–204
Server administrator, **166**
Servers, 109–110
Service, 4
Service level agreement (SLA), 164, 168,
    169
Skill gap analysis, for transition team, 164
SLA, *see* Service level agreement (SLA)
SMEs, *see* Subject matter experts (SMEs)
Software, 1
  initiating process groups, 20
Software bugs, 134

Software development, 1, 7, 41; *see also*
    Agile development methodology
  Agile method for, 1
  costs for, 42
  COTS system, 1–2, 38, 40–41
  custom-developed software, 1, 2
Software development lifecycle (SDLC),
    51–61
  activations, 54
  agile development, 57–58
  case study(ies)
    electronic health record
      implementation, 60, 189–190
    organizational metrics dashboard
      implementation, 61, 190–191
  COTS system, 58–60
  designs, 51, 53
  development phase, 51, 53–54
  incremental model, 57
  inspections, 53
  operations and maintenance phase, 55
  overview, 51
  rapid prototype model, 56–57
  requirements, 51, 52–53
  Spiral model, 56
  stakeholder acceptance and deployment,
    54
  standard phases, 51–52
  testing, 51, 53–54
  validation step, 51, 53–54
  walkthroughs, 53
  Waterfall model, 55–56
Software testing, 133–142
  case study(ies)
    EHR implementation, 141–142,
      204–205
    organizational metrics dashboard
      implementation, 142, 205
  configuration management, 139–141
  cybersecurity testing, 139
  defined, 133
  functional testing, 135
  non-functional testing, 137
  overview, 133–135
  parallel testing, 138–139
  performance testing, 137–138
  regression testing, 137

sample test script, **136**
system integration testing, 136–137
types, 135–139
unit testing, 135
user acceptance testing, 138
Solicitation planning, 47
Spiral Model, 56
Sprints, 68
Stage-gate Reviews, 28
Stakeholder analysis, 94–99, **96**
  focus of energy, 95
  information intake, 95
  life approach, 95–96
  process, 95
Stakeholder management, 2, 48, 91–105
  in action, 103–104
  case study(ies)
    EHR implementation, 104, 194–196
    research tracking system, 104–105,
      196–198
  communication plan, 99–103, **100**
  overview, 91
  stakeholder analysis, 94–99, **96**
  stakeholder identification, 91–94
  stakeholder matrix, 96–98, *97–98*
Stakeholder matrix, 96–98, *97–98*
Stakeholder(s), 7, 21, 25
  acceptance, 54
  committees, 93
  defined, 91
  end-users, 93
  evaluating, 82
  executive leadership, 92
  external resources, 93
  functional/department managers, 93
  identification, 91–94, 161
  project manager, 93, 94–95
  project methodology selection and,
    81–83
  project sponsor(s), 92
  project team, 93
  types of, 92–93
Standard operating procedures (SOPs), 168,
  170
Storage area network (SAN), 110
Subject matter experts (SMEs), 2, 40, 46, 138
Success measurement, 173–180

Agency for Healthcare Research
  and Quality's (AHRQ's) Health
  Information Technology Evaluation
  Toolkit, 176–177
case study(ies)
  EHR implementation, 179, 212–213
  organizational metrics dashboard,
    179–180, 213–214
earned value management (EVM), 174,
  215–217
factors, 174
outcomes, 175–176
outcomes evaluation plan, 177–178
perspectives, 173
Super user(s), **165**
Support center
  characteristics, 157–158
  environment of positive customer
    support, 158
  escalation process, 158
  metrics, 158
  product manager, 158–159
  resources, 158
  strive for first call resolution, 158
System access by outside resources (case
  study), 131, 201–204
System configuration, 107–119
  case study(ies)
    EHR implementation, 118–119, 198–200
    research tracking system
      implementation, 119, 200–201
  client, 108–109
  disaster recovery, 110–112
  environments, 115–118
    considerations, 117–118
    development, 116
    preproduction, 117
    production, 117
    sandbox, 115
    test, 116
    training, 117
  high availability, 112
  interface, 113–115
  network, 112–113
  servers, 109–110
  storage area network (SAN), 110
  workstations, 108

System integration testing, 136–137
Systems and networking administrator, **166**

T

Template(s)
   activation checklist, 244
   agenda-minutes, 235
   Agile requirements management plan, 234
   Agile roadmap, 233
   change request, 242
   communication management plan,
      221–222
   initiation worksheet, 220
   lessons learned, 246–247
   operational readiness review (ORR),
      243
   options document, 239
   post-live issue template, 245
   project charter, 223–228
   project completion analysis document,
      248–249
   project completion document, 250–251
   project roles and contacts, 232
   project scope, 229–231
   project scope change, 240–241
   project status report, 237–238
   user story, 236
Test environment, 116
Testing, 2, 43; *see also* Software testing
   cybersecurity testing, 139
   functional, 135
   non-functional, 137
   parallel testing, 138–139
   performance, 137–138
   regression, 137
   sample test script, **136**
   SDLC, 51, 53–54
   system integration, 136–137
   unit, 135
   user acceptance, 138

Testing lead, **166**
Test plan, 54
Thick/fat client, 109
Thin client, 108–109
Thinnest clients, 109
Timeline, 84
Total cost of ownership (TCO), 160
Training, 117
   user, 144–146
Training lead, **166**
Training plan, 144
Transition to support, 2
Troubleshooting tips/checklist/guidelines,
   169

U

Unit testing, 134, 135
User acceptance testing, 138, 145
User guide, **169**
User story, 68
   template of, 236
User training, 144–146

V

Validation, 43
   SDLC, 51, 53–54
Voice over Internet protocol (VoIP), 164

W

Walkthroughs, 53
Waterfall methodology, 63, 73–75, **86**
   advantages, 74
   disadvantages, 74–75
Waterfall model, 55–56
Web administrator, **166**
Work breakdown structure (WBS), 127
Workstations, 108
Workstations on wheels (WOWs), 113

Printed in the United States
by Baker & Taylor Publisher Services